COOKBOOK
MENUS FOR ALL SEASONS

Canadian Cataloguing in Publication Data
Litwin, Frances J
  President's Choice cookbook: menus for all seasons
Includes index
ISBN 0-9687580-0-2
1. Cookery 2. Convenience foods. 3. Menus. I. Loblaws Inc. II. Title.
TX728.L57 2000   642'.1   C00-931975-1

Loblaws Inc. and its subsidiaries own a number of trademarks including President's Choice®, PC®,
Club Pack®, The Decadent®, Memories of®, Splendido®, Too Good To Be True®, TGTBT, Raisins First®,
The Virtuous®, Italian Magic®, Zipper Back®, Vanilla Decadence, Toasted Coconut Cream Pie Decadence,
Special Occasion, and Eat the Middle First®. Several subsidiaries are licensees of additional trademarks.
These trademarks are the exclusive property of Loblaws Inc. and where used in this cookbook are in italics.
Rustico and Shanghai are trademarks used under license.

A Word About Product Availability

President's Choice® products are available in Canada at Loblaws, Zehrs Food Plus, Zehrs Markets,
no frills, Your Independent Grocer, Fortinos, valu-mart, freshmart, Provigo, Maxi including Maxi & Co.,
Atlantic superstore, Atlantic SaveEasy, SuperValu, Dominion in Newfoundland, the real Canadian
Superstore, the real Canadian Wholesale Club, Extra Foods, Shop Easy Foods, Lucky Dollar Foods and
St. Clair Market. Please note that some products featured in this book may not be available
at all stores. For questions concerning specific products, contact the manager of the store nearest you.

Acknowledgements

The President's Choice cookbook team:
Russell Rudd, Philip Pietrasiak, Randy Bowes, Maria Charvat, Gordana Vulevic, Jason Ha, Michelle Irwin,
Linda Hodgkinson, Alison Kent, Judy Coveney, Melanie Bartel, Ann Quon, Stephanie Fredo

Photography (directed by Russell Rudd): Adrien Duey, David Scott, Douglas Bradshaw
Writer/Editor: Frances Litwin
Recipe Writing: Lesleigh Landry
Wine Consultant: David Lawrason
Production Director: R.W. Pohlak & Associates Inc.
Food Stylists: Denyse Roussin, Josée Robitaille, Ruth Gangbar, Sue Henderson
Set/Prop Stylists: Mireille Lauzon, Janet Walkinshaw, Maggi Jones

Illustration: SharpShooter: Scott McKowen p. 6, 36, 65, 88, 116, 120. Gerard Gauci p. 37, 89, 117-118.
The Stock Illustration Source Inc.: Cover, Jennie Oppenheimer

Stock Photography: Masterfile: Boden, Ledingham p. 10, Alfredo Venturi p. 22, Bill Brooks p. 52, 68,
Mike Dobel p. 67, Travelpix p. 74, Stephen Simpson p. 104. **ImageBank:** Nicolas Russell p. 41,
Ira Montgomery p. 130. **SuperStock:** Garneau, Prevost, Superstock p. 16. Stone: Robert Stahl p. 3,
Joe Cornish p. 46, Michael Orton p. 94, Nicholas DeVore p. 122.

Contents

Introduction

I am proud that the *President's Choice* team has put together such a fantastic cookbook. We believe it is what our customers want.

In an environment where we are all time-pressed, we believe that *President's Choice* products offer the consumer great-tasting, economical, mealtime solutions. And we hear from our customers that the *President's Choice* line provides them with easy entertainment solutions. After listening to you tell us what the *President's* 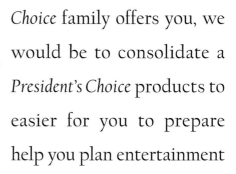 *Choice* family offers you, we decided the logical next step would be to consolidate a variety of our many different *President's Choice* products to see if we could make it even easier for you to prepare meals for your families, and to help you plan entertainment occasions for your friends and guests. That is what gave rise to the notion of doing this cookbook. Knowing, too, that many people wonder how to put a meal together from appetizer to dessert, while others are hard-pressed for time to really plan it out, we wanted to offer you a quick, easy, and hopefully enjoyable experience. The result is a cookbook that is a little bit different from our previous ones in that we've created 16 entire menus – complete from soup to nuts.

In the *President's Choice Cookbook: Menus for All Seasons*, we wanted to show you which combinations of dishes we think are possible. Instead of just recipes, there are menus – a variety of menus ranging from quiet little dinners to festive celebrations. All start with an appetizer and finish with dessert. Then there are the details of the meal to consider – the wine, cheese, bread and coffee or tea you serve with it. Successful meals are built upon such details, so in separate sections throughout the book, we explore the various possibilities open to you.

Why did we choose to do the kind of eclectic menus you find in these pages? Due to various influences – travel, restaurant dining, the incredible increase in television cooking shows – we've all been exposed to a myriad of food ideas that go far beyond what we grew up with in our families. In my family, for example, I was exposed to Swiss and Puerto Rican cuisine. Through these other influences, I've been introduced to Southeast Asian, Oriental and Mediterranean cuisine. What we've attempted to do in Menus for All Seasons is present a variety of complete meals inspired by different cultures around the world, in order to allow you to experiment in a simple and basic way with meal possibilities with which you may be less familiar. Perhaps you already know how to put together an Italian or French meal, but not a Thai dinner. We're hoping this cookbook will provide all of the elements you need to do so.

These menus are not just for guests. We all enjoy making a special meal for our families when time permits – perhaps not on Monday to Friday, but on Saturday or Sunday. I know I look forward to making special meals for my family on weekends. Now that all the planning is done for me, I can tackle that Asian-inspired meal for four (page 22). Or even Cacciucco (Casual Tuscan Supper, page 46), an Italian-style fisherman's soup which brings back fond memories of my holiday trip to Tuscany last summer. What a glorious menu to feed your family on a Sunday! People who love meat and potatoes might venture to try the Hearty Vegetarian Feast (page 80). While I do enjoy meat, I also like to prepare vegetarian meals on occasion, and this meal is one of my favourites.

What we hope we've accomplished with this cookbook is to give you the various meal components to facilitate menu planning, as well as the ease of preparation from using *President's Choice* products – the result being an easy-to-execute meal that should regale your family or guests. Since your feedback and your loyalty to *President's Choice* products were the inspiration for this cookbook, I'd like to dedicate it to you, our customers. This cookbook is your idea. We just put it together.

ROBERT CHENAUX, PRESIDENT, LOBLAW BRANDS LIMITED

Before You Begin...

All of the recipes in the *President's Choice Cookbook: Menus for All Seasons* have been home tested by people just like you – people with all levels of cooking skills. Many of the dishes have been inspired by the cooking of other lands, but they use familiar ingredients (often in offbeat ways) to capture the flavour of a place. There are no culinary absolutes here. It can be an eye-opener to discover that some of the convenience products you see every day at the supermarket can help add an ethnic twist to your dishes. (*Dulce de leche*, for example, made from sweetened condensed milk, is in the words of *PC* Chef Michelle Irwin, "a keeper.") At the same time, we ensure that you don't end up with a lot of more unusual products you only use once – what one well-known British cookbook author has likened to "clothes you never wear, taking up valuable space." And, since in our book the best form of entertaining is the nothing-to-it version, we expect that grocery shopping will be your biggest chore.

A few notes to launch you into a year of cooking fun. Preparation sequence is included with each menu. Make-ahead tips, if possible, are at the end of each recipe. Unless specified, produce is medium size. We don't recommend freezing dishes since the goal of this cookbook is to make it possible for you to prepare an entire menu on the day you intend to serve it.

Cupid's Menu

The cherubic god of love himself, Cupid, presides over this intimate fête. Any son of Venus, let alone a boy god whose name derives from the Latin *cupido*, or desire, makes a good friend on this night. With one well-aimed arrow, pudgy-cheeked Cupid can cause even gods and humans to fall in love. But why ask a boy to do a man's work? So standing in the wings, ready to improve your chances of success, there's trusty St. Valentine, patron saint of lovers since 1381.

Cupid certainly had his quiver full when he planned this menu, stacking the love feast with foods that are rumoured to be aphrodisiacs, although we've no hard evidence that such a thing exists. The textures are varied and sensual – soft, chewy, hard, crunchy, juicy, crackling – and you and your partner must use your hands to partake. Put out your largest napkins!

Menu for 2

Oysters with Mignonette Sauce

Caper-Tomato Cheese Fondue

Strawberries in Chocolate Tuxedoes

Lemon Crush with Minted Sugar

The wine – a sparkling pink
French Champagne or Spanish cava

*Allow 1 1/2 hours. Prepare strawberries.
Bake bread and boil vegetables.
Make mignonette sauce. Cut cooled
bread into pieces. Shuck oysters
and serve. Heat fondue and serve.
Make Lemon Crush.*

The first course is for flirting, and slurping – raw oysters on the half-shell. Casanova regularly ate 50 for breakfast. Being a hermaphrodite, the bivalve is able to experience the best (and worst) of both worlds. Which variety of oyster you shuck will depend on what's in season. By the second course, nothing stands between you except a fondue pot. A third course of chubby strawberries in chocolate jackets and little bow ties won't long be forgotten. Chocolate contains a natural chemical which is supposed to produce a sense of euphoria that's similar to the experience of being in love. Frosty lemon crush is for cooling off.

Should the evening fall short of your expectations, at least you will have had the pleasure of enjoying a special dinner that just happens to look more expensive than it really is.

Caper-Tomato Cheese Fondue

A beautiful rose-hued fondue with little bursts of piquant capers.

1	*PC* Frozen Demi-Baguette Bread (half a 288 g pkg)
1/2 lb (250 g)	tiny new potatoes (about 10), halved
1 cup (250 mL) each	baby carrots, cauliflower flowerets and broccoli flowerets
1 clove	garlic, peeled and slightly crushed
1 pkg (400 g)	*PC* Cheese Fondue from Switzerland
1/3 cup (75 mL)	*PC Splendido* Original *Italian Magic* Sauce
2 tbsp (25 mL)	drained capers

1. Preheat oven to 400°F (200°C). Remove bread from wrapping. Place frozen loaf on baking sheet and bake for 15 to 20 minutes or until golden brown. Cool. Cut into bite-sized pieces.

2. Add potatoes to pot of cold, salted water. Bring to a boil. Boil for 10 to 12 minutes or until tender. Drain.

3. Meanwhile, in separate pan of boiling, salted water, cook carrots for 1 minute. Add cauliflower and continue to boil for 1 minute longer. Add broccoli; cook for 2 minutes longer or until vegetables are tender-crisp. Drain.

4. Rub inside of fondue pot with garlic; discard garlic. Light candle under fondue pot to preheat.

5. In small saucepan, combine fondue, *Italian Magic* and capers. Bring to a boil over medium-high heat, whisking constantly. Transfer mixture to heated fondue pot. Serve with bread and vegetables for dipping.

Makes 2 servings.

Per serving: calories 774; protein 42 g; fat 34 g; carbohydrate 75 g; sodium 1754 mg

Oysters with Mignonette Sauce

Briny oysters are served with fruited versions of a classic accompaniment, mignonette (mee-nyohn-EHT) sauce. Since you need very little, make one sauce now and save the other for your next oyster occasion.

1 dozen	live oysters

RASPBERRY MIGNONETTE SAUCE

1/3 cup (75 mL)	*PC Too Good To Be True* Fat Free Raspberry Dressing
1/4 cup (50 mL)	*PC* Aged Red Wine Vinegar
1 tbsp (15 mL)	finely chopped shallot
1/2 tsp (2 mL) each	salt and coarsely ground black pepper

1. In small bowl, stir together raspberry dressing, vinegar, shallot, salt and pepper. Let stand for 30 minutes.
2. Shuck oysters (see page 141). Top with 1 tsp (5 mL) mignonette sauce and serve.

Mango Mignonette Sauce: In small bowl stir together 1/3 cup (75 mL) *PC TGTBT* Fat Free Mango Dressing, 1/3 cup (75 mL) *PC* Seasoned Rice Vinegar, 1 tbsp (15 mL) finely chopped shallot, 2 tsp (10 mL) *PC* Louisiana Hot Sauce and 1/2 tsp (2 mL) each salt and coarsely ground black pepper. Let stand for 30 minutes.

Makes 2 servings.

Per serving of 6 oysters, each with 1 tsp/5 mL Raspberry Mignonette Sauce: calories 54; protein 4.1 g; fat 1.4 g; carbohydrate 6.3 g; sodium 261 mg

Per serving of 6 oysters, each with 1 tsp/5 mL Mango Mignonette Sauce: calories 67; protein 4.1 g; fat 1.4 g; carbohydrate 7.5 g; sodium 354 mg

Strawberries in Chocolate Tuxedoes

Amusing "stuffed shirts" in handsome chocolate jackets.

15 squares of	*PC* Bittersweet Rich Dark Chocolate (three rows of a 500 g bar), chopped
16 to 20	unhulled strawberries, clean and dry

1. Place chopped chocolate in heatproof bowl.
2. Bring saucepan of water to a boil; remove from heat. Set bowl with chocolate over (not in) hot water. (Water should not touch bottom of bowl). Let stand for 5 minutes, stirring occasionally, or until melted.
3. One at a time, dip back half of strawberries into melted chocolate. Then dip two sides of each berry, leaving front one-quarter plain. Place strawberries chocolate side down on waxed paper-lined baking sheet.
4. Transfer remaining melted chocolate to small resealable plastic bag. With scissors, snip off the tip (just barely, to make the size of a pinhole) from one corner of bag to make a piping bag. Pipe a little bow tie on plain side of strawberry directly beneath leaves, then pipe two or three buttons below. Let strawberries stand in cool place (not refrigerator) for 1 hour, or until chocolate has set.

Variation: Dip only the back half of strawberries into melted chocolate. Pipe parallel lines across plain sides, then pipe a second set of lines at an angle to the first to make a lattice pattern.

Makes 2 servings.

Per serving: calories 437; protein 8.3 g; fat 24 g; carbohydrate 47 g; sodium 6.8 mg

Lemon Crush with Minted Sugar

If you plan to open Champagne, save some for this recipe.

2 tbsp (25 mL)	very finely chopped fresh mint
1 tbsp (15 mL)	granulated sugar
4 scoops	*PC Too Good To Be True* Fat Free Lemon Gelato
1/2 cup (125 mL)	sparkling wine or *PC* White Grape & Peach 100% Juice

1. In small bowl, stir together mint and sugar.
2. Place two scoops gelato into each of two chilled parfait glasses. Drizzle each with 1/4 cup (50 mL) of sparkling wine or fruit juice. Sprinkle with minted sugar.

Makes 2 servings.

Per serving: calories 271; protein 1.9 g; fat 0.4 g; carbohydrate 65 g; sodium 9 mg

A Special Spring Ham

The tradition of serving ham at one of springtime's major celebrations is more of an expression of New World culture than it is of Old World custom. It's how many generations of North Americans have been holding hands with the next. The early settlers relied on hogs (boars are their wild cousin) to provide them with enough meat to last through the winter. Every part of the pig was preserved during the busy harvest season, turned into bacon, ham and sausage, and consumed out of necessity over the following months. By the time springtime and Easter rolled around, most families would still have a ham left in their larder with which to mark the occasion.

To see a handsome ham on the table nowadays, looking resplendent in a shiny glaze, is a rare pleasure; there are so few opportunities in the year to enjoy one. And since hams are already cooked and merely require heating, preparing one is simple – it almost feels like cheating to have such a head start. Indeed, all it takes is a special glaze to make a ham table-worthy. Ham with the bone still in makes the most succulent eating, and ham-lovers swear that the meat that lies closest to it is juiciest and has the most flavour.

Ham is not the only special food that people eat to celebrate the passing of winter and the coming season of vibrant new life. In many countries around the Mediterranean, lamb is served at the paschal observance (from the Aramaic *pashā*, for passover). Regardless of what the springtime celebration is called, or which special foods are eaten, all who mark the occasion with a grateful heart are helping to let go of the past and make room for the new.

Menu for 6

Orange Glazed Holiday Ham with Pan-Roasted Potatoes

Maple Buttered Baby Carrots

Asparagus Salad Platter

Hot Cross Bun Bread Pudding with Apricot-Scented Custard

The wine – a fruity dry white German or Canadian riesling

Allow 4 hours. Bake pudding. Make sauce(s) for pudding; refrigerate. Cook asparagus, hard-boil eggs and prepare greens; refrigerate. Bake ham; add potatoes for last hour. Prepare carrots. Make salad.

Orange Glazed Holiday Ham
with Pan-Roasted Potatoes

*For two, cut the ingredients for the glaze in half and spoon over
a thick ham steak before baking.*

2 cups (500 mL)	*PC* 100% Pure Orange Juice
1/2 cup (125 mL)	*PC* 100% Pure Maple Syrup
1/4 cup (50 mL)	*PC* Finest Seville Orange Marmalade
2 tbsp (25 mL)	*PC* Old-Fashioned Whole Grain Dijon Prepared Mustard
1	*PC Special Occasion* Holiday Half Ham (about 7 lb/3.15 kg)
2 lb (1 kg)	potatoes (about 6 medium), cut in quarters

1. Position rack in centre of oven and preheat to 350°F (180°C).

2. Prepare glaze: In saucepan, combine orange juice, maple syrup, marmalade and mustard. Bring to a boil, stirring. Reduce heat to medium and cook for 15 to 20 minutes or until reduced by about half. Set aside 1/4 cup (50 mL) glaze for potatoes.

3. Remove ham from plastic packaging. If there is a clear plastic guard over the bone, remove it. Trim away desired amount of rind and fat from the surface. Using a sharp knife, make parallel cuts 1-inch (2.5 cm) apart and 1-inch deep (2.5 cm) in surface of ham. Make another series of cuts at an angle to the first to create a diamond pattern. Place ham in roasting pan. Brush generously with some of the glaze.

4. Bake uncovered for 15 to 20 minutes per pound (35 to 45 minutes per kilogram), brushing occasionally with glaze, or until meat thermometer reads 160°F (70°C). In the last hour of cooking, toss potatoes with the reserved 1/4 cup (50 mL) glaze and place around ham. Turn potatoes after 30 minutes in oven.

5. Let ham stand at least 10 minutes before cutting to allow juices to settle back into the meat.

Makes 6 servings, with generous ham leftovers.

Per serving potatoes: calories 117; protein 3.9 g; fat 0.2 g; carbohydrate 25 g; sodium 22 mg

Per 5 oz/150 g glazed ham: calories 224; protein 29 g; fat 5.8 g; carbohydrate 14 g; sodium 1504 mg

Glaze can be made day ahead. Refrigerate. If it thickens too much to brush, reheat in microwave or in saucepan.

Maple Buttered Baby Carrots

The lower moisture content of a Normandy-style butter makes it ideal for cooking and baking.

2 tbsp (25 mL)	*PC* Normandy-Style Salted Butter
4 cups (1 L)	*PC* Frozen Uncommonly Sweet Whole Baby Carrots (half a 1 kg pkg)
2 tbsp (25 mL)	*PC* 100% Pure Maple Syrup
1/4 cup (50 mL)	water
	Salt and freshly ground pepper
1/4 cup (50 mL)	finely chopped fresh parsley

1. In large saucepan, melt butter over medium-high heat. Cook carrots for 3 minutes, stirring.
2. Stir in maple syrup and water. Continue to cook over medium-high heat, stirring occasionally, or until carrots are tender and liquid is absorbed, about 10 minutes.
3. Season to taste with salt and pepper. Add parsley.

Makes 6 servings.

Per serving: calories 85; protein 0.9 g; fat 4.2 g; carbohydrate 11 g; sodium 119 mg

Asparagus Salad Platter

When chives are in bloom, use the violet blossoms as a garnish as well.

24 spears	asparagus, coarse ends trimmed
12	fresh chives
3	hard-boiled eggs
2 cups (500 mL)	torn arugula
2 cups (500 mL)	thinly sliced radicchio
1/2 cup (125 mL)	*PC* Roasted Red Pepper & Goat Cheese Dressing
Pinch each	salt and freshly ground black pepper

1. Cook asparagus for 3 minutes in boiling, salted water, or until tender-crisp; drain. Rinse under cold running water; drain. Gather spears into 6 equal bundles; tie each bundle with a chive. Finely chop remaining chives; reserve.
2. Peel eggs. Using fingers, gently break egg whites and remove whole yolks. Keeping separate, grate whites and yolks.
3. In large bowl, toss arugula and radicchio with dressing. Arrange salad on serving platter. Place bundles of asparagus on top of salad, spacing evenly apart. Scatter grated eggs between bundles, alternating between whites and yolks.
4. Sprinkle with chopped chives, salt and pepper.

Makes 6 servings.

Per serving: calories 119; protein 5.3 g; fat 8.5 g; carbohydrate 5.4 g; sodium 308 mg

Hot Cross Bun Bread Pudding with Apricot-Scented Custard

Our alternative sauce, a brandied apricot sauce, is bursting with tangy fruit flavour.

1 pkg (525 g, 8 buns)	*PC Raisins First* Hot Cross Buns
3/4 cup (175 mL)	*PC Too Good To Be True* Twice the Fruit Apricot Spread
3	eggs
2 cups (500 mL)	10% cream
1/4 cup (50 mL)	*PC* 100% Pure Maple Syrup
1 can (425 g)	*PC* Devon Custard

Brandied Apricot Sauce: In medium bowl, combine 1/2 cup (125 mL) *PC TGTBT* Twice the Fruit Apricot Spread, 1/2 cup (125 mL) *PC* 100% Pure Maple Syrup and 1 tbsp (15 mL) brandy.

Per 2 tbsp/25 mL of Brandied Apricot Sauce: calories 72; protein 0 g; fat 0 g; carbohydrate 18 g; sodium 4.6 mg

Per 2 tbsp/25 mL of Apricot-Scented Custard: calories 33; protein 0.9 g; fat 0.8 g; carbohydrate 5.6 g; sodium 16 mg

1. Position rack in centre of oven and preheat to 350°F (180°C). Spray 8-inch (2 L) round or square baking dish with cooking spray.

2. Cut hot cross buns in half horizontally. Spread bottom halves with 1/2 cup (125 mL) of the apricot spread; replace tops. Cut buns in quarters; arrange tightly in double layer in prepared dish, tops facing up.

3. In bowl, whisk together eggs, cream and maple syrup. Pour over buns. With a wooden spoon, press down on buns to make sure the entire top layer gets soaked in cream mixture.

4. Bake for 50 to 60 minutes, or until top is deep golden and pudding is set. Serve warm or at room temperature with sauce of choice.

5. **Apricot-Scented Custard:** In medium bowl, whisk together Devon custard and remaining 1/4 cup (50 mL) apricot spread. Serve as is, or warm in saucepan over medium heat for 3 to 5 minutes, stirring frequently.

Makes 6 servings.

Per serving pudding, without sauce: calories 410; protein 14 g; fat 14 g; carbohydrate 57 g; sodium 347 mg

Pudding and sauce can be made night before. Cover and refrigerate. Return pudding to room temperature, or reheat at 325°F (160°C) for 20 minutes.

A Taste of Asia

It helps if cooks know the food preferences and dislikes of their guests before presenting exotic dishes as a *fait accompli*. It's simply easier on everyone's nerves. No one has to hide their face behind a napkin, or decide that going out to a restaurant might be a better idea after all.

However, a menu which tastes of all things Far Eastern – soya sauce, Peking duck, ginger and green tea – is one of the cookbook team's personal favourites. It received high marks from our home testers, too, for tasting delicious over-all and being very straightforward to prepare. We anticipate that most people with inquisitive palates will delight in the fusion of flavours offered here. The presentation is decidedly Japanese in feeling from start to finish.

The dinner perfectly illustrates the "fusion" phenomenon which has seen many chefs inspired to enrich their own cuisines with ingredients and techniques borrowed from other cultures. Smoked salmon is a Western food, yet in this menu it strikes up a companionable partnership with mango and seasoned sticky rice. Of course, the duck noodle stir-fry with Asian-style vegetables starts with an advantage – pasta, in the form of plump udon noodles. The granita intrigues because the icy crystals burst with unexpected ginger and green tea essence instead of the usual fruit flavours.

Fusion cooking requires a deft touch, as flavours should not be so startling that people wonder about your judgment. Happily, there are enough familiar tastes here to ensure that guests leave the table well-pleased at having eaten something so exciting.

Menu for 4

Smoked Salmon Sushi with Mango

Memories of *Kobe Beef Yakitori*

Citrus-Soya Dipping Sauce

Udon Noodles with Hoisin Peking Duck Stir-fry

Vinegared Cucumber Salad

Gingered Green Tea Granita

The wine – an off-dry white *riesling, muscat or gewurztraminer*

Make granita 5 1/2 hours ahead. Allow 2 1/2 hours for meal. Make salad and dipping sauce; refrigerate. Cook rice. Soak skewers. Bake duck. Make sushi and assemble skewers; refrigerate. Make stir-fry (don't add duck yet); keep warm. Grill beef skewers. Finish stir-fry.

Udon Noodles with Hoisin Peking Duck Stir-fry

The sauce that comes with the Peking duck steps up the flavour of this noodle stir-fry.

1 pkg (396 g)	*PC* Frozen Peking Duck
1 pkg (350 g)	*PC* Udon Japanese-Style Noodles
2 tbsp (25 mL)	*PC Memories of Shanghai* Stir-fry Oil
1/2 cup (125 mL)	*PC Memories of* The Han Dynasty Stir-fry Sauce
Half	large white onion, cut in wedges
1 pkg (375 g)	*PC* Frozen *Shanghai* Stir-fry Vegetables

1. Preheat oven to 375°F (190°C). Remove packet of hoisin sauce from Peking duck package. Place duck in shallow baking tray on middle rack of oven. Bake for 35 to 40 minutes if frozen or 15 to 20 minutes if thawed, or until internal temperature is 160°F (70°C). Pull meat and skin from bones in small shreds.

2. In large pot of boiling water, cook noodles for 4 minutes; drain. Rinse under cold running water; drain. Toss with 1 tsp (5 mL) of *Memories of Shanghai* oil.

3. In small bowl, stir together *Memories of* the Han Dynasty sauce and hoisin sauce.

4. In wok or large frying pan, heat 1 tbsp (15 mL) of *Memories of Shanghai* oil over high heat. Stir-fry onion and frozen vegetables for 4 to 5 minutes. Add shredded duck meat and sauce mixture; stir-fry for 3 minutes or until heated through. Remove from heat. Keep warm.

5. In frying pan, heat remaining *Memories of Shanghai* oil over high heat. Add noodles; cook for 3 to 5 minutes, stirring, or until heated through. Divide among four bowls. Top evenly with vegetable-duck mixture.

Makes 4 servings.

Per serving: calories 586; protein 28 g; fat 20 g; carbohydrate 73 g; sodium 1125 mg

Thawing duck overnight in refrigerator speeds preparation.

Smoked Salmon Sushi with Mango

If desired, you can tuck tiny balls of green wasabi paste, a hot Japanese horseradish, underneath the pieces of smoked salmon.

1 tbsp (15 mL)	granulated sugar
2 tbsp (25 mL)	*PC* Seasoned Rice Vinegar
1 cup (250 mL)	raw *PC* Medium-Grain Sticky Rice, freshly cooked according to package instructions
1/4 cup (50 mL)	chopped ripe mango
1 pkg (150 g)	*PC* Bay of Fundy Smoked Atlantic Salmon
1/4 cup (50 mL)	pickled ginger
2 tbsp (25 mL)	wasabi paste (optional)

1. In small bowl, dissolve sugar in vinegar. Stir into rice. Set rice aside to cool.

2. Wet hands with cold water. Place 2 tbsp (25 mL) of cooled rice mixture into palm of one hand. Make a hollow. Place one piece of mango in hollow. Shape into a ball, pressing rice around mango. Place on platter. Repeat with remaining rice and mango.

3. Drape a small piece of smoked salmon over each rice ball. Place pickled ginger and, if desired, wasabi on platter. Serve with Citrus-Soya Dipping Sauce.

Makes 4 servings (16 sushi).

Per serving: calories 266; protein 11 g; fat 5.1 g; carbohydrate 44 g; sodium 582 mg

Memories of Kobe Beef Yakitori

The Japanese word "yakitori" has come to mean any small piece of food that is skewered and grilled (yaki), not just chicken (tori).

1 lb (500 g)	flank steak
12	wooden skewers, soaked 1 hour
1/3 cup (75 mL)	*PC Memories of* Kobe The 2 Minute Miracle Tamari Garlic Marinade
1	green onion, finely sliced

1. Preheat barbecue to medium high. Lightly oil grill.
2. Slice steak across the grain in 1/2-inch (1 cm) wide strips. Thread steak onto skewers. Brush with marinade. Let stand for 2 minutes.
3. Cook for 2 to 3 minutes per side or until desired doneness. Transfer to platter. Sprinkle with green onion. Serve with Citrus-Soya Dipping Sauce.

Makes 4 servings.

Per serving: calories 207; protein 26 g; fat 9.8 g; carbohydrate 3.8 g; sodium 768 mg

Citrus-Soya Dipping Sauce

A Japanese-style ponzu sauce for the sushi and beef yakitori.

1/4 cup (50 mL)	*PC* Naturally Brewed Soya Sauce
1/4 cup (50 mL)	*PC* 100% Pure Orange Juice, pulp free
1/4 cup (50 mL)	fresh lemon juice
2 tbsp (25 mL)	*PC* Seasoned Rice Vinegar

1. In small bowl, whisk together soya sauce, orange juice, lemon juice and vinegar. Makes 3/4 cup (175 mL).

Makes 4 servings.

Per serving: calories 20; protein 0.1 g; fat 0 g; carbohydrate 4.9 g; sodium 810 mg

Vinegared Cucumber Salad

You can serve these mildly spicy cucumber slices with many home-cooked dishes.

1/4 cup (50 mL)	*PC* Seasoned Rice Vinegar
2 tbsp (25 mL)	*PC* Premium Alfalfa Honey
2 tsp (10 mL)	*PC Memories of* Thailand Fiery Thai Dipping Sauce
1 tsp (5 mL)	*PC* Pure Sesame Oil
1/4 tsp (1 mL)	salt
1	English cucumber, cut in paper-thin slices
1 tsp (5 mL)	sesame seeds

1. In large bowl, whisk together vinegar, honey, sauce, oil and salt. Add cucumber; toss to coat. Chill until serving. Serve sprinkled with sesame seeds.

Makes 4 servings.

Per serving: calories 77; protein 1.3 g; fat 1.3 g; carbohydrate 15 g; sodium 188 mg

Can be made night before. Refrigerate.

Gingered Green Tea Granita

The beguiling flavour and icy green sparkle make this dessert a winner.

4 cups (1 L)	water
1/2 cup (125 mL)	granulated sugar
1 tbsp (15 mL)	grated peeled fresh gingerroot
4 tea bags	*PC* Green Tea

1. In saucepan, combine water, sugar and ginger. Bring to a boil. Remove from heat. Add tea bags. Cover and let stand 10 minutes.

2. Strain mixture into 8-inch (2 L) cake pan. Place in freezer. Freeze for 2 hours. Stir. Return to freezer for another 3 hours, or until mixture is slushy but not frozen solid. (If mixture freezes solid, let stand at room temperature for 5 to 10 minutes, then lightly pound with ice cream scoop until slushy.) Spoon into dessert bowls.

Makes 4 servings.

Per serving: calories 108; protein 0 g; fat 0 g; carbohydrate 27 g; sodium 7.4 mg

Mother's Day Brunch

The best advice a mother can give a child who invades her kitchen is, "Never apologize for anything you cook." (It makes the guests uncomfortable.) Fortunately, mom won't have to worry about burnt offerings when her family prepares this elegant and very pretty brunch. The parent charged with overseeing the activity, and reinforcing the cardinal rule of always reading a recipe over twice before starting, should find it very doable.

There have been festivals celebrating motherhood since time immemorial. The ancient Phrygians in the Near East declared Cybele, daughter of heaven and earth, to be mother of all gods. The Romans called her Magna Mater – Great Mother or All-Nurturing One. The ritual with which we're familiar, that of presenting flowers and special cakes, dates back to the Middle Ages, when the English were obliged to visit their church once a year to honour the spiritual power that protected them from harm. Mothering Sunday gave children who lived with their employers a chance to return home for the day to spend time with their families.

The second Sunday of May was officially set aside for honouring North American mothers in 1914 by a U.S. president. South Africans, who like to say, "The hand that rocks the cradle rules the nation and its destiny," celebrate motherhood on the first Sunday in May. The French celebrate it on the last Sunday of the month. Though dates may differ from one country to the next, the sentiment is the same: To pay respect to the one who every child knows is responsible for making the sun go to bed at night.

Menu for 6

Fruit Salad in Orange Cups

―――――

Scrambled Egg Puddings with Mustard and Smoked Salmon

―――――

Spring Salad with Mango Dressing

―――――

Lemon Poppyseed Cream Cheese Streusel Coffee Cake

―――――

Iced Lemon & Ginger Mint Tea

―――――

The wine – a sparkling white Italian prosecco

Allow 2 1/2 hours. Make tea; refrigerate. Bake cake. Prepare salad greens and salmon rosettes; refrigerate. Assemble fruit salad cups. Finish salad. Make egg puddings.

Scrambled Egg Puddings with Mustard and Smoked Salmon

Creamy eggs in delicate Yorkshire puddings are as genteel as Mother.

1 pkg (150 g)	PC Bay of Fundy Smoked Atlantic Salmon
6	eggs
1/3 cup (75 mL)	10% cream
1/4 tsp (1 mL)	each salt and freshly ground black pepper
1 pkg (185 g)	PC Frozen Yorkshire Puddings
2 tbsp (25 mL)	PC Old-Fashioned Whole Grain Dijon Prepared Mustard
1 tbsp (15 mL)	unsalted butter
	Dill sprigs

1. Position rack in centre of oven and preheat to 400°F (200°C).
2. Divide salmon into 12 pieces. Roll up to resemble roses.
3. In bowl, whisk together eggs, cream, salt and pepper.
4. Place frozen Yorkshire puddings on baking sheet. Spread mustard evenly inside each pudding. Bake for 4 minutes.
5. Meanwhile, in large heavy-bottomed pan, melt butter over medium heat. Add egg mixture. Cook for 5 minutes, stirring slowly, or until eggs are cooked. Divide scrambled eggs among Yorkshire puddings.
6. Place salmon roses on top of scrambled eggs. Garnish with dill.

Makes 6 servings.

Per serving: calories 260; protein 16 g; fat 16 g; carbohydrate 13 g; sodium 654 mg.

Spring Salad with Mango Dressing

Lightly dressed spring greens make a nice side salad for these brunch puddings. Candied peanuts add a surprise crunch.

In serving bowl, toss together 1 head Boston lettuce, torn into bite-sized pieces; 1 bunch watercress, thick stems removed; 1 1/2 cups (375 mL) orange segments reserved from fruit cups (see page 35) and 1/3 cup (75 mL) *PC Too Good To Be True* Fat Free Mango Dressing. Sprinkle with 1/3 cup (75 mL) *PC* Butter Toffee Peanuts, crushed.

Makes 6 servings.

Per serving: calories 100; protein 2.8 g; fat 2.8 g; carbohydrate 16 g; sodium 55 mg

Lemon Poppyseed Cream Cheese Streusel Coffee Cake

An enchanting creation. Homey, moist and very delicious.

8 oz (250 g)	cream cheese, softened for 30 minutes at room temperature
1/3 cup (75 mL)	granulated sugar
3	eggs
1 tbsp (15 mL)	finely grated lemon rind
1 tbsp (15 mL)	fresh lemon juice
1 tsp (5 mL)	almond extract
1 pkg (465 g)	*PC* Lemon Poppyseed Coffee Cake Mix
1 tbsp (15 mL)	unsalted butter, softened
2/3 cup (150 mL)	water
1/3 cup (75 mL)	*PC The Virtuous* Canola Oil

1. Position rack in centre of oven and preheat to 325°F (160°C). Spray 9-inch (2.5 L) springform pan with cooking spray.

2. In bowl and using electric mixer, beat cream cheese with sugar until smooth. Beat in one egg, lemon rind, lemon juice and almond extract. Set aside.

3. Empty streusel mix packet into a small plastic bag; add butter. Rub and press contents together in bag until mixture is uniformly blended.

4. In large bowl, combine cake mix, water, oil and remaining two eggs. Using electric mixer, beat on low speed until moistened. Increase speed to medium low and beat one minute longer. Pour half of cake batter into prepared pan. Pour cream cheese mixture evenly over batter. Top with remaining cake batter. Sprinkle with streusel.

5. Bake for 55 to 60 minutes, or until top is golden and cake springs back when lightly pressed. Cool in pan on rack for 10 minutes. Remove from pan; cool on rack. Serve warm or at room temperature.

Makes 8 servings.

Per serving: calories 413; protein 10 g; fat 17 g; carbohydrate 55 g; sodium 423 mg

Fruit Salad in Orange Cups

Passion fruit juice brightens up a classic brunch opener.

3	large navel oranges
1 container (750 mL)	*PC* Fruit Salad in Passion Fruit Juice Syrup
6	strawberries

1. Cut oranges in half crosswise. Cut a thin slice from the bottom of each orange half as necessary to make it sit securely on a plate. Loosen flesh with knife. Using tip of spoon, carefully remove flesh from orange halves, reserving hollowed-out cups.

2. Separate orange flesh into segments. Reserve 1 1/2 cups (375 mL) of segments for Spring Salad (see page 32); place remainder in bowl along with fruit salad and juices.

3. Using a slotted spoon, divide fruit salad mixture among orange cups. Garnish each with a strawberry.

Makes 6 servings.

Per serving: calories 97; protein 0.9 g; fat 0.2 g; carbohydrate 23 g; sodium 17 mg

Iced Lemon & Ginger Mint Tea

The combination of flavours in this beverage spell pure refreshment.

4 tea bags	*PC* Moroccan-Style Green Tea with Mint
8	thin slices fresh gingerroot, unpeeled
1/2 cup (125 mL)	loosely packed whole fresh mint leaves
1/2 cup (125 mL)	granulated sugar
6 cups (1.5 L)	boiling water
1/2 cup (125 mL)	fresh lemon juice
6	sprigs fresh mint (optional)

1. Place tea bags, ginger, mint and sugar in saucepan. Pour in boiling water. Cover and let stand for 10 minutes.

2. Strain tea into large pitcher. Stir in lemon juice. Refrigerate for 2 hours or until cold.

3. Pour into ice-filled glasses. If desired, garnish with mint.

Makes 6 servings.

Per serving: calories 92; protein 1.3 g; fat 0.3 g; carbohydrate 21 g; sodium 8 mg

The Bread Basket

Before meat, or even potatoes, there was bread. Until the last century, bread was 'the' single most important food no matter what your station in life. Now bread is a detail of the meal, and still no less essential. Food critics will judge restaurants by the quality of their bread because it makes the first impression. They don't wait to see how the menu reads, or even what's on the wine list.

We've learned to appreciate the value of a great loaf of bread, the one with perfect crust, crumb and taste – the kind of honest loaf that would have cost 16th-century French workers the equivalent of half their daily wages. The so-called artisan breads, full of fresh whole grains, are the best thing since...well, sliced bread. Yet specialty breads aren't anything new, according to food historians. The Egyptians excelled at fancy baked goods. The Greeks had 72 sorts of breads available to them, which used every grain and method of baking known at the time.

Throughout history, all sorts of grains have been used to make bread, especially wheat, rye, millet, oats, corn and barley. In general, the higher you rose in society, the less you ate of dark grains like rye or whole wheat. Sweet breads, such as hot cross buns or Italian panettone, are celebration breads. From the beginning, these enriched breads were made with only the finest wheat flour, so they would be light in texture, flavour and appearance.

The desire to make bread is exceeded only by our desire to eat it. In the home, the smell of fresh baked bread warm from the oven or the bread machine seems to cry out, "Come right in. Join us, please!"

During medieval times, many people bought their bread ready-made from guild bakers who were equipped to grind the grain but loathe to share their recipes. During that period, dense bread "trenchers" served as dinner plates. (Those trenchers were the original "chargers" or underplates of today – the large, beautifully decorated plates that are whisked away in restaurants almost as soon as you sit down.) More bread was provided for general eating. Bread, cheese and fruit always preceded the first course.

Crusty rye, peasant bread, multi-grain, flaxseed bread – the bread counter is a veritable file of cultural favourites. Other types of bread contribute to our existence, too, especially flatbreads. The wrap, inspired by the Mexican wheat flour tortilla, is a popular choice for sandwiches. The corn tortilla comes to us flat, folded and baked crisp for tacos, and as corn chips for dipping into salsa. Bread sticks or straws add crunch to a meal and height to a table setting when you fill a container with them. (Wrapped with prosciutto and laid on a plate beside a slice of melon, they make a tasty starter to enjoy with drinks.)

As for crackers, people have been eating them since they were flint-hard, flour-and-water rations. Crackers are the bread of travellers, as valuable as gold in times of sailing ships and wagon trains. When the ship Arbella pulled away from England's shores in the 1600s with the Puritans, there were 20,000 crackers in the hold. Just the expression "cracker barrel days" evokes an entire chapter in the history of North America.

The rise of bread

Yeast is what raises bread dough. These microscopic, plant-like organisms feed on starches in flour, converting the sugars to carbon dioxide bubbles that cause the bread to expand and rise. There is already some yeast to be found in fresh whole grains, which are the basis of the first artisan breads. True artisan bread is subject to the vagaries of yeast because it's traditionally leavened solely by free-roaming yeasts found naturally in the air, or by incorporating "starters" such as spongy ferments called sourdough or a piece of dough held back from the previous mix – what the French call levain.

Before commercial yeasts arrived on the scene about 50 years ago, bread was made from sour dough or an even more fickle ferment made from corn. Yeast spores also inhabit kneading troughs in which bread dough is mixed, and which are still used in many of the older bakeries in France today. By the time the flour-and-liquid mixture is worked to a soft dough, it often will have picked up sufficient yeast to help it rise.

Bread machine yeasts are an even more recent innovation than commercial yeast. And they are the executives of the yeast world, compared to other varieties available. These quick-dissolving, fine, dry-yeast granules do their job smartly and efficiently, with none of the over-the-top yeasty flavours that were a problem with active dry yeasts even as little as 10 years ago, which put many people off baking their own bread at home.

Heat from the oven stops yeast's activity.

For best keeping

A quality loaf of bread from the store, the oven or a bread machine can keep well for a day or two at room temperature, unwrapped, cut side down on the bread board. By day two, you may wish to loosely wrap the rest of the uneaten loaf in the wrapper it came in to help hold in moisture.

Breads with thick crusts tend to keep better, because the crust acts as a protective barrier, helping to keep the insides of the loaf from drying out. Rye breads stay moister longer. To rejuvenate a crusty, artisan bread and restore its bakery-fresh flavour, sprinkle with water and heat at 250°F (120°C) for 5 to 10 minutes.

Bread, and especially sweet breads, generally freeze well. What you need to remember about most breads is this: the longer they take to freeze and to thaw, the more their flavour suffers. So don't feel it's necessary to keep the loaf intact. *PC* Artisan Breads can be frozen whole (more on that later), but if in doubt, abide by the small-is-better rule. To promote rapid freezing and protect eating quality, cut the bread into slices, or split smaller breads such as English muffins in halves and then reassemble, before freezing in an airtight bag, such as a heavy-duty, resealable plastic bag. (If you're so inclined, use a straw to suck out the last bit of air from the bag.) Then it's simply a matter of pulling out the number of slices or muffin halves you require. You can pop frozen bread or muffins straight into a toaster, or leave a few slices out overnight, loosely wrapped in waxed paper, to enjoy at breakfast.

President's Choice Artisan Breads are suitable for home freezing, provided you wrap them well. Defrost for one hour at room temperature. For a crisp crust, bake the unwrapped, defrosted loaf directly on the middle oven rack at 375°F (190°C) for 5 to 8 minutes.

In the beginning...

Fresh bread cries out for fresh butter. But you might also want to try "Italian butter" – olive oil! Here's a simple but tasteful starter for an Italian dinner. Place a ribbon of grated Parmesan cheese down the centre of bread plates. Pour *PC Splendido* Extra Virgin Olive Oil on one side and a *PC* flavoured olive oil of your choice on the other. Now drizzle each of the oils with a bit of *PC* 8-Year-Old Balsamic Vinegar. To eat, dip a piece of crusty Italian bread into some of the oil-vinegar mixture, swirling to meld the two, and then into the cheese.

A funny thing about bagels...

The first recorded mention of bagels, in 1610, comes from Cracow, Poland. However, here's an interesting piece of lore that has some food historians scratching their collective head. How did a bread that looks and tastes very much like a bagel end up in northwestern China among the Uighur, one of the oldest Turkic-speaking peoples of Central Asia? Apparently, they've been making and eating a bagel-like flatbread for thousands of years. Bagels have been found in their tombs dating to about 100 AD. There is a possibility that Jewish merchants travelling to the Orient might have shared the recipe for making their favourite bread (its roundness symbolic of unending life). Or else the bread travelled from East to West.

What To Do With The Leftovers

Fresh bread is best consumed straightaway. But unless there are enough people to eat it, leftover bread is inevitable. But these are not annoying leftovers. The remains of a loaf can be cut into cubes and used for stuffing, made into golden toast baskets, or turned into breadcrumbs for casserole toppings. Here are some suggestions for what to do with bread. For more ideas, refer to your favourite all-purpose cookbook.

Bread Salad: Bread salad is the frugal conclusion to a next-day loaf in many cultures. In Italy, bread salad is made with stale bread soaked in water, then squeezed dry. The bread is torn into pieces, then tossed with tomatoes, herbs, olive oil and vinegar. The bread adds texture and helps soak up the flavours of the dressing and the juices released from the vegetables. Pita bread is used in Middle Eastern bread salads.

Bruschetta: At its simplest, bruschetta is garlic toast: thick slices of peasant-style bread toasted on the grill, rubbed with a clove of garlic and drizzled with olive oil. The name derives from the Italian *bruciato*, or burned.

Toast Baskets: Also called croustades, these little containers can be made with any thinly sliced, white bread – nothing fancy. Trim off the crusts and roll each slice with a heavy rolling pin. Brush both sides lightly with melted butter and press into muffin cups – the right size for filling with scrambled eggs or other savoury filling for a light lunch. (Or cut out small rounds with a biscuit cutter and press into mini muffin tins to make appetizer-sized baskets, to be filled with vegetable dips or bruschetta topping.) Bake at 275°F (140°C) for a few minutes, until they just turn golden. Toast baskets can be made a day ahead, and stored in an airtight container at room temperature.

Quick Canapes: Trim crusts from sliced bread and cut into 2-inch (5 cm) squares. Toast in the oven. Spread with herb- or mustard-flavoured butter, or spread thinly with egg, tuna or salmon sandwich fillings.

Pita Toasts: Nice for dipping, and for nibbling on. Brush pita rounds lightly with extra-virgin olive oil; sprinkle with herbs or seeds, and cut into wedges. Bake at 400°F (200°C) for about 4 minutes or until they start to colour. They will become crispy when they cool.

Breadcrumbs: Pulse in a food processor until you have light, fluffy, fresh crumbs. Italian cooks often sauté fresh breadcrumbs in some olive oil until golden, then toss them with seafood and pasta to add texture to the dish. Fresh breadcrumbs are the basis for English bread sauce, which is served with goose or turkey. For a few spoonfuls of breadcrumbs, run a stale loaf over a hand grater.

The Gaucho Grill

The mere thought of South American-style barbecue is enough to whet the appetite since already the emphasis is on hearty eating. Were it not for the pastel prettiness of Lime Tango Coolers, which guests can sip while the lamb sizzles, and the sumptuousness of Coconut Cream Parfaits with caramelly *dulce de leche* topping, this menu could have been created by a hungry Argentinian cowboy owing to the chimichurri sauce which, next to salt, is a gaucho's best friend. Green with herbs and sharp with vinegar, chimichurri is always served with rich meats such as grilled lamb or beef. The only debate revolves around whether the consistency should be smooth or chunky, and people are as much sticklers for one or the other as Canadians are about how they prefer to have their peanut butter.

Our reinvention of the gaucho grill takes in a broad sweep of Latin flavours from Central and South America and the Caribbean islands. A ceviche-style appetizer draws inspiration from the purist's approach – cooking raw fish in citrus juices – and a contemporary Salvadoran home version made with tomato soup. The succession of courses, with make-ahead steps built in, affords you and your guests a spirited journey through lands stamped with Latin food traditions – the rich dowry bequeathed by Spanish and Portuguese conquests in the New World. Even the Irish have a toehold in our panorama since they, along with the Basques, originally controlled sheep-farming in Patagonia, a popular tourist region that lies south of Argentina's bustling capital of Buenos Aires. All in all, you're in for an exciting taste adventure!

Menu for 6

Ceviche-Style Shrimp

Chimichurri Lamb with Pineapple Salsa

Roasted Sweet Potatoes

Coconut Cream Parfait with Dulce de Leche

Lime Tango Cooler

The wine – a full mellow red *Argentine malbec*

Thaw shrimp in refrigerator overnight. Allow 2 1/2 hours for meal. Marinate lamb. Make dulce de leche topping. Prepare shrimp appetizer. Put lamb on grill. Prepare potatoes. Prepare salsa. Assemble parfaits; freeze. Make Lime Tango Coolers.

Chimichurri Lamb with Pineapple Salsa

Made with vinegar, garlic, herbs and dried chilies, chimichurri sauce is the ketchup of South America.

1	boneless, butterflied leg of New Zealand lamb (about 2 1/2 lb/1.25 kg)
1 1/4 cups (300 mL)	*PC Memories of* Patagonia Herb & Garlic Chimichurri Sauce
1 1/2 tsp (7 mL)	salt
Half	pineapple, peeled, cored and cut in thick rings
1	red onion, thickly sliced into rounds
1/4 cup (50 mL)	chopped fresh coriander

1. In shallow glass baking dish, coat lamb with 1/2 cup (125 mL) of the chimichurri sauce. Cover with plastic wrap. Let stand at room temperature for 1 hour.

2. Preheat barbecue to medium. Lightly oil grill.

3. Remove lamb from marinade and discard any sauce remaining in dish. Sprinkle lamb with salt. Place on grill; close lid. Cook for 40 to 50 minutes, turning every 10 minutes and basting with 1/2 cup (125 mL) of the chimichurri sauce, or until internal temperature registers 130°F (54°C) for medium-rare. Remove to serving platter and cover loosely with foil. Let stand 10 minutes.

4. While lamb rests, toss pineapple and onion in remaining 1/4 cup (50 mL) chimichurri sauce. Cook on grill for 8 to 10 minutes, turning once, or until tender. Chop into 1/2-inch (1 cm) cubes. Toss with coriander in serving bowl.

5. Slice lamb thinly across the grain. Serve with warm salsa.

Makes 6 servings, with leftovers of lamb.

Per 5 oz/150 g serving of lamb with salsa:
calories 337; protein 42 g; fat 15 g;
carbohydrate 8.5 g; sodium 591 mg

Lamb can be marinated overnight.
Refrigerate. Return to room
temperature before cooking.

Ceviche-Style Shrimp

Cooked shrimp get their Latin American flair from lime, herbs, tomato and onion. Dig in – use your fingers!

1 bag (454 g)	*PC* Frozen Cooked Black Tiger Shrimp (51-60 count), thawed and drained
1/2 cup (125 mL)	diced red onion
1/4 cup (50 mL)	chopped fresh coriander
2 tbsp (25 mL)	chopped fresh chives
1/2 cup (125 mL)	*PC Splendido* Original *Italian Magic* Sauce
1/4 cup (50 mL)	*PC* Roasted Red Pepper Dip
2 tbsp (25 mL)	fresh lime juice
	Fresh chives (optional garnish)

1. Place shrimp in bowl, leaving tails on. Stir in red onion, coriander and chives.

2. In another bowl, whisk together *Italian Magic*, red pepper dip and lime juice. Pour over shrimp mixture; toss to coat.

3. Cover shrimp with plastic wrap. Chill for 1 hour. Serve on a bed of chives or in martini glasses.

Makes 6 servings.

Per serving: calories 97; protein 15 g; fat 2.6 g; carbohydrate 3.3 g; sodium 143 mg

Can be prepared night before.

Lime Tango Cooler

You can make this tropical beverage and the dulce de leche *parfait topping (see recipe next page) with one 398 mL can of coconut milk. (Stir the coconut milk well after opening.)*

3/4 cup (175 mL)	*PC* Key Lime Sherbet
1 1/3 cups (325 mL)	coconut milk
1/3 cup (75 mL)	fresh lime juice
1/4 cup (50 mL)	dark rum (optional)
3 cups (750 mL)	*PC* Sparkling Lemonade (or two 355 mL cans)
	Lime slices

1. In blender, combine sherbet, coconut milk, lime juice and rum, if using. Purée for 45 seconds or until smooth. Just before serving, add sparkling lemonade. (Do not blend.)

2. Pour into ice-filled glasses. Top with some of the creamy froth, and serve garnished with lime slices.

Makes 6 servings.

Per serving: calories 235; protein 1.0 g; fat 11 g; carbohydrate 33 g; sodium 20 mg

Base of drink can be prepared 2 hours ahead. Refrigerate. Add sparkling lemonade just before serving.

Roasted Sweet Potatoes

The potato skins add a rustic look but are still tender enough to eat.

3	sweet potatoes (skin on)
2 tbsp (25 mL)	fresh lime juice
2 tbsp (25 mL)	PC Roasted Garlic Flavoured Olive Oil
1/2 tsp (2 mL) each	salt and freshly ground black pepper

1. Preheat oven to 375°F (190°C).

2. Cut sweet potatoes into 1/2-inch (1 cm) thick rounds.

3. In bowl, toss sweet potatoes with lime juice, oil, salt and pepper. Spread onto large rimmed baking sheet. Bake for 15 minutes. Turn slices. Bake another 15 minutes, or until tender and lightly browned.

Makes 6 servings.

Per serving: calories 197; protein 2.6 g; fat 4.7 g; carbohydrate 36 g; sodium 209 mg

Coconut Cream Parfait with Dulce de Leche

Dulce de leche (DOOL-seh deh LEH-cheh) means "milk sweet" in Spanish. This pudding-like caramelized milk is eaten for dessert and even as a breakfast spread in South and Latin America.

1 can (300 mL)	PC Sweetened Condensed Milk
or 1 1/4 cups (300 mL)	PC Gourmet Butterscotch Ice Cream and Dessert Topping
1/3 cup (75 mL)	coconut milk (omit if using butterscotch topping)
4	PC Meringue Nests, coarsely crumbled
12	small scoops PC Toasted Coconut Cream Pie Decadence Ice Cream

1. Position rack in centre of oven and preheat to 425°F (220°C).

2. For *dulce de leche:* Pour condensed milk into 8-inch (2 L) square baking dish; cover pan tightly with foil. Set dish in larger pan; pour in enough boiling water to come half way up the sides of baking dish. Bake for 1 1/2 hours, topping up with boiling water after 45 minutes. Remove dish from water bath and uncover. Let cool for 30 minutes, then gradually whisk in coconut milk.

3. Divide half of crumbled meringues among six parfait glasses or brandy snifters. Top with a small scoop of ice cream. Drizzle half of *dulce de leche* over ice cream. (Alternatively, use butterscotch topping.) Repeat layers. Serve immediately.

Makes 6 servings.

Per serving: calories 470; protein 8.1 g; fat 18 g; carbohydrate 69 g; sodium 164 mg

Parfaits can be made day ahead. Store in freezer.

A Casual Tuscan Supper

About an hour out of Rome by car, heading north on the A1 toward Florence, the regional capital of Tuscany, one finally waves goodbye to the fields of sunflowers being grown for their oil and arrives in the land of the poet Dante. The vista becomes increasingly one of gently rolling hills of green and gold, terra-cotta rooftops, and olive-treed slopes.

Even at the height of summer, the days never feel too hot in Tuscany. By nightfall, the temperature dips to a refreshing coolness, allowing one to rest comfortably in the passing breeze from an open window. Perhaps you have never been to Tuscany. But you have brushed up against its history if you have ever heard the Gregorian chant recorded by monks at the Abbey of Sant'Antimo in the Tuscan hills...medieval ruins with gloomy corridors that are in stark contrast to the sunny brightness of the rest of this region in northern Italy, with its green freshness and meandering, cypress-lined roads.

To put you and your guests one step closer to this delightful part of Italy – in spirit, at least – we propose a casual but showy seafood supper that's a breeze to pull together. Since one of Tuscany's provinces lies along a virtual extension of the Riviera, this menu pays homage to both the land and the sea. It satisfies with aromatic rosemary in both the appetizer and the Cacciucco (apparently tasting all the better if you include a stone from a sea bed), the lush vibrancy of ripe tomatoes in an uncooked pasta sauce, and fresh berries splashed with balsamic vinegar and paired with the flavour of burnt almond chocolate.

Menu for 6

Marinated Goat Cheese served with Crusty Italian Bread

Pasta Fresca

Cacciucco (Fisherman's Soup)

Bittersweet Almond Chocolate Cake with Balsamic Strawberries

The wine – a light red
young Chianti or Tuscan sangiovese

Thaw shrimp and salmon in refrigerator overnight. Allow 2 1/2 hours for meal. Bake cake. Prepare appetizer, berries and seafood; chill. Prepare vegetables. Transfer appetizer to table. Bake bread. Start soup (don't add seafood). Make toast and pasta. Finish soup.

Cacciucco (Fisherman's Soup)

Rosemary perfumes this cacciucco (kah-CHOO-ko), whose name means "mixture." Legend says a fisherman's widow first made it for her children from leftover catches begged from other fishermen.

3 tbsp (45 mL)	*PC Splendido* Extra Virgin Olive Oil
3	large leeks, white part only, finely sliced
4 cups (1 L)	cold water
1 bottle (660 mL)	*PC Splendido* Onion & Garlic *Italian Magic* Sauce
1/2 cup (125 mL)	dry white wine
3 tbsp (45 mL)	finely chopped fresh rosemary
6	large slices Italian bread
2	*PC* Frozen Atlantic Salmon Skinless Fillets, thawed, cut lengthwise in half, then crosswise into 1-inch (2 cm) pieces
1 bag (454 g)	*PC* Frozen Uncooked *Zipper Back* Large Black Tiger Shrimp (31-40 count), thawed, peeled and tail on
1 lb (500 g)	live mussels

1. In large saucepan, heat oil over medium-low heat. Add leeks; cover and cook for 10 minutes, stirring occasionally, or until soft. Do not brown.

2. Stir in water, *Italian Magic*, wine and rosemary. Cover; reduce heat to low.

3. Preheat broiler. Arrange bread on baking sheet. Toast in oven under broiler for 1 to 2 minutes, or until golden brown.

4. Bring tomato mixture to a boil. Stir in salmon, shrimp and mussels. Cover and cook for 3 to 5 minutes, or until shrimp have turned pink and mussels have opened. (Discard any unopened mussels.)

5. Serve soup with toasted bread.

Makes 6 servings.

Per serving: calories 349; protein 20 g; fat 13 g; carbohydrate 38 g; sodium 946 mg

Soup may be made day ahead to point of adding rosemary. Refrigerate.

Marinated Goat Cheese
served with Crusty Italian Bread

If olive oil is the lifeblood of Tuscan cuisine, bread is the foundation. And anything eaten with bread, such as this easily assembled savoury appetizer, is called companatico.

1 pkg (140 g)	*PC* Soft Unripened Goat's Milk Cheese
6	black olives, pitted and chopped
3	oil-packed sun-dried tomatoes, chopped
1 tbsp (15 mL)	finely chopped fresh rosemary
2 tbsp (25 mL)	*PC Splendido* Extra Virgin Olive Oil
1 tbsp (15 mL)	*PC* 8-Year-Old Balsamic Vinegar Freshly ground black pepper
1 pkg (280 g)	*PC Rustico* Crusty Italian-Style White Bread, baked according to package instructions

1. Cut goat cheese crosswise into 1/2-inch (1 cm) slices. Arrange on serving plate.

2. In bowl, mix together olives, tomatoes, rosemary, olive oil and vinegar. Season to taste with pepper. Pour over goat cheese. Refrigerate, covered, for at least 1 hour.

3. Return goat cheese to room temperature before serving with thin slices of *Rustico* bread.

Makes 6 servings.

Per serving: calories 131; protein 3.8 g; fat 12 g; carbohydrate 3.1 g; sodium 236 mg

Can be made day ahead.
Refrigerate.

Pasta Fresca

An uncooked pasta sauce makes perfect summer eating.

1 1/2 cups (375 mL)	*PC Splendido* Cavatappi Pasta
2 tbsp (25 mL)	*PC* Roasted Garlic Flavoured Olive Oil
7 slices	*PC* Fully Cooked Bacon (half a 65 g pkg), chopped
3 cups (750 mL)	chopped arugula or spinach leaves
2 cups (500 mL)	grape or cherry tomatoes (about 1 pint), cut in half
1/2 cup (125 mL)	chopped fresh basil
1/3 cup (75 mL)	*PC Splendido* Grated 100% Italian Parmesan Cheese (optional) Freshly ground black pepper

1. In large pot of boiling, salted water, cook cavatappi for 8 minutes or until tender but firm. Drain. Place in bowl with garlic oil and bacon; toss to coat.

2. Add arugula (or spinach), tomatoes, basil and, if desired, Parmesan; toss until well mixed. Season with black pepper to taste.

Makes 6 servings.

Per serving (without cheese): calories 154; protein 5.4 g; fat 7.2 g; carbohydrate 17 g; sodium 127 mg

Bittersweet Almond Chocolate Cake with Balsamic Strawberries

A tempting little chocolate cake – delicious, uncomplicated and like many Italian cakes, not a high riser. Balsamic vinegar intensifies the flavour of strawberries, an Italian cook's trick.

1/2 cup (125 mL)	granulated sugar
2 tbsp (25 mL)	water
Half	a 400 g bar *PC* Dark Almond Rich Bittersweet Chocolate, chopped
1/3 cup (75 mL)	*PC* Normandy-Style Unsalted Butter, cubed
2	eggs
1/3 cup (75 mL)	all-purpose flour
2 cups (500 mL)	sliced fresh strawberries
1 tbsp (15 mL)	*PC* 8-Year-Old Balsamic Vinegar
1 tbsp (15 mL)	*PC* Premium Alfalfa Honey
	Sifted icing sugar

1. Position rack in centre of oven and preheat to 350°F (180°C). Spray 8-by-4-inch (1.5 L) nonstick loaf pan with cooking spray.

2. In small, heavy-bottomed saucepan, combine sugar and water. Cook over medium-high heat for 3 minutes, stirring occasionally (sugar won't dissolve completely). Reduce heat to low. Stir in chocolate and butter; cook for 3 to 5 minutes, stirring constantly, or just until melted and smooth. Remove from heat.

3. In large bowl and using electric mixer, beat eggs with flour until smooth. Beat in chocolate mixture. Pour into prepared pan. Bake for 25 to 30 minutes or until toothpick inserted in centre comes out with a few moist crumbs attached. Cool in pan on rack.

4. Meanwhile, in bowl, toss together strawberries, vinegar and honey.

5. Turn out cake by inverting pan. Cut crosswise into six slices.

6. Divide prepared strawberries among six dessert plates, top with a slice of cake and sprinkle with icing sugar.

Makes 6 servings.

Per serving: calories 428; protein 7.3 g; fat 23 g; carbohydrate 48 g; sodium 23 mg

The Hottest Night Of The Year

It's so hot it makes the head swim. There's a drone in the air, insects buzzing their endless, repetitive, monotonous song of summer. The heat of the day carries its perfume for blocks. It's almost too much to bear, you think, wilting in the heat and growing light-headed with the smells of the mown grass, the blossoms, the fragrance coming from the rose arbour. Secretly, you take delight in soaking up the hot, sweaty, intangible loveliness of summer. Just when you get close to grasping its essence, it slips away, steals away from you, feet fast-tripping across the yard, past the gate, down the street and then it's gone...

Whoahh! If you didn't have anything better to do than take it easy and put your feet up in a deck chair, you'd enjoy the reverie. But you've already invited the guests over so you had better get busy. You won't be using the oven today, however; it's too hot to fire up anything but the outdoor grill. And there will be no spicy foods this evening, either; it's bound to be pretty sultry as it is. Your reward for taking the heat is an easy little dinner that's all about cool, colour and crunch...from the sliced ripe tomatoes and a slaw that almost makes itself, to the shrimp brochettes that require the briefest of assembly (and no long marinating, but instead a quick brush of flavour as they cook).

And the best is saved for last. Honest-to-goodness, summer pudding that requires none of the painstaking effort that's usually invested in preparing the berries for this traditional English dessert. Yes, with chilled double cream to spoon over! If that doesn't whet heat-dulled appetites, then nothing will.

Menu for 4

Tomato Feta Basil Salad

Citrus Shrimp Brochettes

Summer Slaw

Summer Berry Pudding with Double Cream

The wine – a medium mellow white *Canadian or Oregon pinot gris*

Make summer pudding day ahead. Thaw shrimp in refrigerator overnight. Allow 1 hour for meal. Soak skewers. Prepare summer slaw. Prepare tomato salad. Assemble brochettes; grill.

Citrus Shrimp Brochettes

People of the Mediterranean know that seafood requires minimal anointing to taste its best.

1 bag (454 g)	*PC* Frozen *Zipper Back* Jumbo Shrimp (21-30 count), thawed and peeled, tail on
8	wooden skewers, soaked 1 hour
1	zucchini (skin on), cut in half lengthwise, then crosswise into 8 pieces
Half	lemon, cut in 8 small wedges
1/2 cup (125 mL)	*PC Too Good To Be True* Fat Free Citrus Basil Dressing

1. Preheat barbecue to medium high. Lightly oil grill.

2. Thread one shrimp lengthwise onto skewer, followed with one zucchini piece, a lemon wedge, another zucchini piece and another shrimp. Repeat with remaining shrimp, zucchini and lemon wedges. Use up all of the shrimp (some skewers will have three shrimp).

3. Brush brochettes generously with dressing. Place on grill; close lid. Cook for 3 minutes per side or until shrimp are opaque. Serve on top of summer slaw.

Makes 4 servings.

Per serving: calories 79; protein 9.2 g; fat 0.5 g; carbohydrate 9.5 g; sodium 174 mg

Tomato Feta Basil Salad

Yellow tomatoes taste more mellow than the red variety.

1/4 cup (50 mL)	*PC* Roasted Garlic Balsamic Low Fat Vinaigrette
2	yellow tomatoes, thickly sliced
2	red tomatoes, thickly sliced
Half	a 175 g pkg *PC* Goat's Milk Feta Cheese in Brine, drained and cut lengthwise into 4 to 8 slices
1/2 cup (125 mL)	loosely packed fresh basil leaves
	Salt and freshly ground black pepper

1. Drizzle half of vinaigrette over four salad plates. Place tomato slices on vinaigrette. Arrange feta and basil attractively on top of tomatoes. Sprinkle with salt and pepper to taste. Drizzle remaining vinaigrette evenly over top.

Makes 4 servings.

Per serving: calories 126; protein 5.8 g; fat 6.1 g; carbohydrate 12 g; sodium 314 mg

Summer Slaw

The cool crunch and look of this slaw is an antidote for fatigue.

2	sweet yellow peppers, cut in thin slivers
2 cups (500 mL)	shredded red cabbage
3	green onions, thinly sliced
1/2 cup (125 mL)	*PC Memories of* Szechwan Peanut Sauce and Dressing
1/2 cup (125 mL)	*PC Too Good To Be True* Fat Free Plain Yogurt

1. In bowl, toss yellow peppers, red cabbage and green onions.
2. In another bowl, whisk sauce and yogurt. Pour over vegetables; toss to coat.

Makes 4 servings.

Per serving: calories 195; protein 6.2 g; fat 8.2 g; carbohydrate 24 g; sodium 360 mg
Vegetables and dressing can be prepared separately day ahead. Refrigerate.

Summer Berry Pudding with Double Cream

One taste of this English-style dessert will convince guests you own the berry patch.

10 to 12 slices	good quality Italian bread, cut 1/2-inch (1 cm) thick, crusts removed
1 pkg (600 g)	*PC* 6-Berry Frozen Fruit Blend, thawed
1/2 cup (125 mL)	*PC* 100% Pure Orange Juice, pulp free
1/2 cup (125 mL)	packed brown sugar
Half	250 mL tub *PC* Fresh, Thick Double Cream

1. Line 4- to 6-cup (1 to 1.5 L) bowl with plastic wrap, leaving a 5-inch (12 cm) overhang all around.

2. Line bowl with some of the bread, cutting pieces as necessary to fit.

3. In saucepan, combine fruit blend, orange juice and brown sugar. Bring to a boil, stirring. Reduce heat to medium-low; simmer for 6 to 8 minutes, stirring occasionally. Pour hot mixture into bread-lined bowl. Trim excess bread even with fruit mixture.

4. Cover fruit with bread slices, cutting pieces as necessary to fit. Bring plastic overhang up over top to cover pudding completely. Place small plate on top of pudding. Top with heavy cans or another weight. Refrigerate overnight.

5. Remove weight and plate. Unwrap plastic from top of pudding. Place serving platter over bowl and carefully invert onto platter. Remove bowl and plastic wrap. Using serrated knife, carefully cut pudding into wedges. Serve with cream.

Makes 6 servings.

Per serving with 2 tbsp/25 mL double cream:
calories 332; protein 5.5 g; fat 14 g; carbohydrate 46 g; sodium 255 mg

Pudding must be prepared the night before.

The Backyard Barbecue

Hold up a mirror to the past and what do you see? The backyard barbecue – the very best of summer! When cooking with charcoal reached the pinnacle of suburban acceptance in the 1950s, barbecuing wasn't confined to people's backyards. Many Canadians will recall seeing a side of beef spit-roasting in a farmer's field on the weekends. All summer long, families out for a drive could stop for barbecue and help the civic-minded organization sponsoring the event raise money for a worthy cause.

Like the old-fashioned carousel at the amusement park, the backyard barbecue is associated with good times. There's something about firing up the grill that seems to slow the pace of life. Barbecuing becomes a time to slip into leisure mode, and with this easy, updated menu, even the cook gets a chance to settle into that lazy feeling.

From start to finish, the menu redefines what you can do on the grill. Here the love of barbecue finds its modern-day expression in barbecued Brie – the flavours and textures will bring guests to their senses – and a central platter that respects the vegetable as well as the meat. What better way to give thanks for the season's early vegetable bounty than by letting the grilled vegetables tower over their companions on the plate? Note there's no steer on this plate but pork, since we're still in the midst of a white-meat renaissance. (The garlicky tzatziki that accompanies it wouldn't have been known in the '50s, except as a food memory brought home from Greece.) In place of the usual ice-cream offerings, there are spiced fruit sundaes in edible containers.

Menu for 4

Relish-Topped Barbecued Brie

Grilled Herbed Pork Tenderloin
with Tzatziki

Grilled Vegetable Towers

Grilled New Potato Salad

Spiced Fruit Sundaes in Meringue Nests

The wine – a chilled light red
Beaujolais or Canadian gamay

Thaw fruit in refrigerator overnight. Allow 2 1/2 hours for meal. Parboil potatoes. Grill potatoes. Grill vegetables. Assemble Bries (do not grill) and towers. Finish potato salad. Make fruit topping. Grill Brie and pork. Assemble dessert.

Grilled Herbed
Pork Tenderloin with Tzatziki

Garlicky tzatziki, made with yogurt, adds another layer of flavour to grill-ready marinated pork tenderloin.

1	*PC* Garden Pepper and Herb Marinated Pork Tenderloin (about 1 1/4 lb/625 g)
	PC Splendido Extra Virgin Olive Oil
1/2 cup (125 mL)	*PC Too Good To Be True* Fat Free Tzatziki Dip and Spread

1. Preheat barbecue to medium. Lightly oil grill.
2. Cook tenderloin for 20 to 25 minutes, turning occasionally and brushing lightly with oil if it sticks, or until internal temperature is 160°F (70°C) and juices run clear when pork is pierced.
4. Slice on the diagonal. Serve with tzatziki.

Makes 4 servings.

Per serving: calories 181; protein 35 g; fat 2.5 g; carbohydrate 4.7 g; sodium 717 mg

Relish-Topped Barbecued Brie

Warmed Brie carries an appetizing zing.

4-inch (10 cm)	wheel of Brie
2 tbsp (25 mL)	*PC* Zesty Tomato-Pepper Relish
2 tbsp (25 mL)	*PC* Lemongrass Corn Relish
1 bag (142 g)	*PC* Rosemary Olive Oil Potato Chips

1. Preheat barbecue to medium.
2. Carefully cut away top rind of Brie. Cut wheel in half to make two semi-circles. Top one semi-circle with tomato relish, the other with corn relish.
3. Place one semi-circle in the centre of 8-inch (20 cm) square of foil. Bring edges of foil up around sides and gather above Brie, without letting foil touch relish. Repeat with other piece of Brie.
4. Place packets on barbecue; close lid. Cook for 4 to 6 minutes, partially unwrapping to check if Brie has softened. Carefully turn foil down around base of Brie (do not remove from foil). Place warmed Bries on serving platter, and surround with piles of chips.

Makes 4 servings.

Per serving: calories 389; protein 16 g; fat 25 g; carbohydrate 25 g; sodium 575 mg

Brie packets can be assembled day ahead to point of grilling. Refrigerate.

Grilled Vegetable Towers

These herb-speared stacks add excitement to a plate.

4	sprigs fresh rosemary
1	zucchini
2	sweet peppers (red and yellow)
1	eggplant
1/3 cup (75 mL)	*PC* Italian Dressing
Pinch each	salt and freshly ground black pepper

1. Preheat barbecue to medium. Lightly oil grill.
2. Remove and discard leaves from bottom 2 inches (5 cm) of rosemary sprigs.
3. Trim zucchini; slice on diagonal into 8 pieces. Core peppers. Cut each pepper into quarters, then cut each quarter in half diagonally to make 8 pieces. Cut 4 rounds of eggplant, each 1/2-inch (1 cm) thick.
4. Toss vegetables with dressing, salt and pepper. Transfer to grill. Cook zucchini for 9 minutes, peppers for 11 minutes, and eggplant for 13 minutes, turning occasionally, or until tender. Let cool.
5. Using eggplant slices as the base, form four stacks, dividing vegetables evenly. Spear each stack with bare end of rosemary sprig. Serve at room temperature.

Makes 4 servings.

Per serving: calories 111; protein 1.6 g; fat 8.0 g; carbohydrate 8.2 g; sodium 304 mg

Towers can be prepared 2 to 3 hours ahead. Let stand at room temperature, loosely covered.

Grilled New Potato Salad

Creamy on the inside, slightly smoky on the outside.

1 lb (500 g)	small new potatoes, cut in half (about 10)
1 tbsp (15 mL)	*PC Splendido* Extra Virgin Olive Oil
1 cup (250 mL)	cherry tomatoes, cut in half
1/3 cup (75 mL)	*PC* Fat Free Honey Dijon Dressing
3	green onions, sliced

1. Preheat barbecue to medium high. Lightly oil grill.
2. Place potatoes in saucepan of cold, salted water. Bring to a boil. Cook for 10 to 12 minutes or until tender. Drain. Toss with oil.
3. Grill potatoes for 8 to 10 minutes, turning occasionally until charred. Transfer to bowl. Toss with tomatoes, dressing, and green onions. Serve warm or at room temperature.

Makes 4 servings.

Per serving: calories 163; protein 3.7 g; fat 4.0 g; carbohydrate 28 g; sodium 587 mg

Can be made 2 to 3 hours ahead. Cover and let stand at room temperature.

Spiced Fruit Sundaes in Meringue Nests

Spices add mystery to a fruit topping.

1/3 cup (75 mL)	*PC* 100% Pure Maple Syrup
1 tsp (5 mL)	vanilla
1/4 tsp (1 mL) each	ground ginger and freshly grated nutmeg
1 tbsp (15 mL)	unsalted butter
1 tub (600 g)	*PC* Peach-Strawberry-Rhubarb Frozen Fruit Blend, thawed
4	*PC* Meringue Nests
4 scoops	*PC Vanilla Decadence* Ice Cream

1. In bowl, whisk together maple syrup, vanilla, ginger and nutmeg.
2. In large frying pan, melt butter over medium heat. Stir in maple syrup mixture. Cook for 2 minutes, stirring occasionally. Stir in fruit blend. Return to simmer; cook for 5 minutes, stirring occasionally. Remove from heat.
3. Fill each nest with a scoop of vanilla ice cream. Spoon fruit mixture over ice cream.

Makes 4 servings.

Per serving: calories 352; protein 4.2 g; fat 11 g; carbohydrate 59 g; sodium 48 mg

Remember to thaw fruit blend overnight in refrigerator.

The art of wine-matching

Explore. Follow whims. Take advice... reject advice!

That's the most comfortable approach to take towards wine, according to wine consultant and educator David Lawrason, who suggested the wines for the menus in this cookbook. "More important than finding the perfect match every time is building a repertoire of tastes that you enjoy, like growing a CD collection," he says. "The best way to organize your collection of tastes is by wine styles, not by countries of origin or even grape varieties. Styles govern personal preferences, food matches, how long wine should age, serving temperature – just about everything of any importance when it comes to getting the most out of wine."

There are two underlying principles at work every time you put food and wine together on the table, he says. "First, wine must refresh and keep your palate on that craving edge. Wines with prominent acidity refresh well, as do wines with bubbles and wines served at cooler temperature, including reds. Even that dry, puckery tannin in younger reds can help saw through rich flavour build-up. Second, the wine and food should weigh in at equal levels of flavour intensity (strong or weak) and textural density (thick or thin). It's all a question of balance, of live and let live. Why waste a delicately nuanced recipe by completely over-matching it with a brute of a wine, or vice versa? After that, find the common flavour references in both the recipe and wine description. And voila, it should work."

There's reason for optimism – you have a lifetime to play around with food and wine combinations. "If you start enjoying wine each night with dinner at age 25 and cease somewhere at around age 75, you'll have about 18,000 occasions to match food and wine," David says. "Even if you only enjoy wine on weekends, that's close to 5,000 opportunities."

Follow along these next few pages as David Lawrason steers a straight course through the often overwhelming world of wines...

Find Your Wine Style

The Europeans label and market by region because they long ago discovered which grapes best fit various regions to create an identifiable regional taste. The New World gang added a confusing twist – labelling by grape variety – because they are trying all the combinations and can't use European place names. Neither approach adequately identifies the style of wine in the bottle, which is actually the most practical way to buy and use wine. So for newcomers, the chart below cross-references styles – in increasing order of weight and flavour intensity – to the major grape varieties, where they originate, and foods with which they're compatible.

The style chart quickly pinpoints what styles and grapes Canada does best, thanks to our cooler, northerly climate. Overall, our wines have much more to do with central European styles than those of California, Chile or Australia. By and large, they're terrific with food because they possess that palate-cleansing acidity. Canada began turning things around in the 1980s by planting the right family of vinifera (European) grapes, and then, in 1988, banning native labrusca varieties like concord from table wine. The same year, the industries in Ontario and British Columbia put together the Vintners Quality Alliance or VQA, a now legislated program of standards for 100 per cent Canadian-grown and bottled wine. It also created official VQA wine-growing appellations based on the European model.

Styles	Grape Varieties	Major Regions	Food Fit
WHITES			
sparkling	diverse	Champagne, Loire, Spain	hors d'oeuvre
light crisp whites	auxerrois, muscadet, Italian	France, Canada, Italy	white fish
medium herbal whites	sauvignon blanc, semillon	Loire, Bordeaux, New Zealand	vegetarian, salads
medium mellow whites	pinot blanc, pinot gris	Alsace, Canada, Oregon	pork, poultry
fruity, aromatic whites	riesling, gewurztraminer, muscat	Germany, Alsace, Canada	Asian, pork
rich oak-aged whites	chardonnay	Burgundy, New World	grilled white meats
REDS			
dry rosés (blush)	grenache, (white) zinfandel	France, Spain, New World	picnics
light unoaked reds	gamay	Beaujolais, Canada	poultry, ham
light oaked reds	pinot noir	Burgundy, Canada, Oregon	turkey, salmon
medium lively reds	sangiovese, tempranillo	Chianti (Italy), Rioja (Spain)	pasta, pizza
medium mellow reds	merlot, cabernet franc	Bordeaux, California, Canada	burgers, ribs
heavy dry reds	cabernet sauvignon	Bordeaux, all New World	lamb, steaks
heavy mellow reds	syrah (shiraz), zinfandel	Rhone, Australia, California	richest meats
AFTER DINNER			
late harvest, dessert	riesling, semillon	Germany, Canada, Sauternes	fruit, cheese
icewine	vidal, riesling, gewurztraminer	Canada, Germany	flans, pies
fortified sweet	various	port, cream sherry	chocolate, nuts

Six Great Serving Tips

How much to buy

Most people can easily and safely consume one-third to one-half bottle during a three-course meal, and more as the number of courses and duration increases. Fill glasses half full for each course (about 4 oz/125 mL). Don't forget half bottles for solo and couple dining, or the great fun of magnums for large groups.

Chill out, warm up

We North Americans consistently drink whites too cold (robbing flavour) and reds too warm (robbing refreshment). No wine should be served at room temperature if your room is over 65°F (18°C). Increase temperature with the increasing weight of the wine (see chart). Start at about 40°F (4°C) for sparkling and sweet dessert wines, then ranging up to 63°F (17°C) for the richest reds and fortifieds. To chill, submerge in ice water; to heat, submerge in lukewarm water.

Hurrah for heavy breathing

Wine aromas change and become more generous when exposed to oxygen. Simply pulling the cork and letting the wine stand in the bottle exposes very little wine to oxygen. Forget it. For real heavy breathing, which thoroughly mixes oxygen, decant reds into a broad-based decanter for 30 to 90 minutes, depending on lighter or heavier style. If it's an old red wine or port with sediment, decant gently to keep the dregs trapped in the bottle. Decant whites right into the glass so they don't warm in the process.

Corked wine and other bad stuff

Flawed wine is not your fault! Don't be embarrassed, do not let it spoil the party. Turn it into education for those who might be interested in identifying the wet cardboard smell of a corked wine, the burnt match of sulphur dioxide, or the dill-pickle vinegar of acetic acid. Always have a back-up bottle on hand, and return the offender for refund the next day (obviously, with some contents remaining).

Water guests very well

As a responsible host, make sure liberal quantities of still mineral water are available at all times. Guests will drink water instead of wine to slake thirst, reducing their actual alcohol intake. Water also continually flushes the system and combats the dehydrating effects of alcohol, the leading cause of hangover.

Storing leftovers

Your best wine preserver is your refrigerator. It should keep opened whites and reds fresh enough to drink for up to four days, maybe longer for young wines and fortified wines. Rewarm reds if necessary in lukewarm water and re-breathe by pouring into the glass. Forget preserving gizmos with valves and pumps. Buy the canisters that spray an inert, colourless, tasteless, environmentally friendly and oxygen-proof gas blanket into the bottle. After repouring, let wine breathe in the glass five minutes.

The Wine Cellar as Spice Rack

Wherever possible, store wine in a constant, cool, dark, slightly humid environment. If you are storing expensive age-worthy reds out of financial or sentimental investment, go all out on a custom-built, fine wine cellar. If you simply want an assortment of styles on hand that serves much like a spice rack, to enjoy no matter the recipe or who is showing up for dinner, you should stock about 75 bottles – but not in the kitchen. If your home doesn't naturally have a cool spot, invest in a small, stand-alone, temperature-controlled wine cabinet. (You'll never regret the expense). Do not store wines near your stove, radiators, on top of kitchen cupboards or below well-travelled staircases.

A Meal to Delight Friends

Fly fishermen consider the salmon a worthy challenge. Such an agile fish, so beautiful with its sparkling, quicksilver skin which provides camouflage at sea, an awesome creature possessed of imponderable energy...

In Nature's hands, the salmon spends much of its life in cold ocean waters or deep lakes before returning to fresh water to spawn. One of the largest salmon ever recorded – 79 pounds, 2 ounces (35.89 kg) – was caught in a river in Norway back in 1928, in an age when salmon who were following their extraordinary genetic imperative for regular transatlantic runs were much more plentiful in the world.

It is a victory to win a salmon for the table, where it is considered a luxury food even to this day, although you no longer have to catch your own. (There are people who harvest them.)

Menu for 4

Minted Pea Soup

———

Salmon Roast with
Tomato-Olive Sauce

———

Couscous with Green Beans

———

Warm Phyllo-Wrapped Cheesecakes
with Raspberry-Orange Sauce

———

The wine – a lighter red
pinot noir or Valpolicella

Thaw salmon and phyllo in refrigerator
overnight. Allow 1 1/2 hours for meal.
Purée soup; set aside.
Assemble desserts (do not bake);
freeze. Make raspberry sauce.
Bake salmon; make sauce. Make couscous.
Reheat soup. Bake desserts.

Our Atlantic salmon comes already dressed and stuffed for the occasion. So the cook is spared the effort of having to find a whole fillet, and then making a spinach-and-feta-cheese filling over which it can be folded. The flavours of the salmon roast are mild and pleasing, and the entrée is an easy one to build on. Since this dinner warrants a sit-down format, there's a minted pea soup to start. The grain called couscous is intimidating in name only. Essentially, it's pasta, and if you can bring water to a boil, you can make couscous. Time saved on the main course can now be put to use making a truly stunning dessert using individual cheesecakes and phyllo pastry, which itself takes only about 20 minutes of real work.

The lure is provided. Now you can decide who to reel in ...

Salmon Roast with Tomato-Olive Sauce

The Mediterranean-style sauce complements the spinach-and-feta-cheese stuffing. Plum tomatoes have a meaty flesh.

1 pkg (650 g)	*PC* Frozen Stuffed Atlantic Salmon with Spinach and Feta Stuffing, thawed (see Note)
1 tbsp (15 mL)	*PC Splendido* Extra Virgin Olive Oil
1	shallot, finely chopped
10	black olives, pitted and chopped
1	plum tomato, roughly chopped
1/4 cup (50 mL)	chopped fresh parsley
1/2 tsp (2 mL)	fresh lemon juice

1. Cook thawed salmon roast according to package instructions.

2. In frying pan, heat oil over medium-high heat; cook shallot for 2 minutes, stirring frequently, or until translucent. Do not brown. Stir in olives, tomato, parsley and lemon juice. Cook for 1 minute or just until heated through. Serve warm or at room temperature.

3. Carefully remove netting from salmon roast. Slice crosswise into four portions. Serve with sauce spooned over top.

Makes 4 servings.

Note: See package instructions for cooking from frozen.

Per serving: calories 360; protein 25 g; fat 24 g; carbohydrate 11 g; sodium 421 mg

Couscous with Green Beans

The sweetness of Vidalia onions accents this mild-tasting dish.

1 1/4 cups (300 mL)	water
1 cup (250 mL)	*PC Memories* of Marrakech Couscous
1 tbsp (15 mL)	*PC Splendido* Extra Virgin Olive Oil
1/4 tsp (1 mL)	salt
2 cups (500 mL)	halved, trimmed green beans
3/4 cup (175 mL)	*PC Too Good To Be True* Fat Free Tomato & Vidalia Onion Dressing
1/2 cup (125 mL)	pine nuts (optional, see Note)

1. In saucepan, bring water to a boil. Stir in couscous, oil and salt. Remove from heat. Cover and let stand for 5 minutes. Fluff with a fork. Cool.
2. In pot of boiling, salted water, cook green beans for 3 to 4 minutes or until tender-crisp. Drain. Rinse under cold running water; drain. Toss with 1/4 cup (50 mL) of the dressing and half of pine nuts, if using.
3. Stir remaining dressing and pine nuts, if using, into cooled couscous. Transfer to serving platter. Arrange green beans over couscous.

Makes 4 servings.

Note: Place roughly chopped pine nuts on rimmed baking sheet and bake in preheated oven at 375°F (190°C) for 3 to 5 minutes, watching closely, or until golden and fragrant. Cool.

Per serving, without pine nuts: calories 258; protein 7.4 g; fat 4 g; carbohydrate 48 g; sodium 277 mg

Minted Pea Soup

Fresh mint adds a lively freshness and extra boost of colour.

1 tbsp (15 mL)	*PC* Fresh Concentrated Chicken Stock
2 1/2 cups (625 mL)	boiling water
2 tbsp (25 mL)	*PC The Virtuous* Canola Oil
6	green onions, chopped
3 cups (750 mL)	*PC* Frozen Petits Pois
1/4 cup (50 mL)	chopped fresh mint
	Salt and freshly ground black pepper

1. Dissolve chicken stock concentrate in boiling water.
2. In large saucepan, heat oil over medium heat. Cook green onions for 5 minutes or until softened.
3. Stir in peas and chicken stock. Bring to a boil. Immediately remove from heat and add mint. Purée in batches in blender or food processor. Return to saucepan and reheat gently over medium heat, stirring. Season to taste with salt and pepper.

Makes 4 servings.

Per serving: calories 168; protein 7.1 g; fat 7.5 g; carbohydrate 18 g; sodium 454 mg

Can be prepared day ahead to point of reheating. Refrigerate. Reheat gently without boiling.

Warm Phyllo-Wrapped Cheesecakes with Raspberry-Orange Sauce

A stunning dessert made with frozen miniature cheesecakes.

4 sheets	*PC* Frozen Phyllo Pastry, thawed
3 tbsp (45 mL)	unsalted butter, melted
1 pkg (4 x 100 g)	individual *PC* Frozen Original New York-Style Cheesecakes (do not thaw)
3/4 cup (175 mL)	*PC* Raspberry Freezer Jam
1/3 cup (75 mL)	*PC* 100% Pure Orange Juice

1. Position rack in centre of oven and preheat to 400°F (200°C).

2. Brush one sheet of phyllo with melted butter. Top with another sheet of phyllo; brush with butter. Cut phyllo stack in half crosswise. Repeat with remaining two phyllo sheets. You will have four stacks.

3. Place one frozen cheesecake in centre of each phyllo stack. Top each cheesecake with 1 tbsp (15 mL) raspberry jam. Draw phyllo up around cheesecake and pinch together above jam. Packet will resemble a drawstring purse. Brush all over with remaining butter. Transfer to baking sheet.

4. Bake for 10 to 12 minutes or until phyllo is golden and crisp.

5. Raspberry-Orange Sauce: In saucepan, stir together orange juice and remaining jam. Bring to a boil over medium-high heat, stirring. Reduce heat to medium; cook for 3 to 5 minutes or until slightly thickened. Remove from heat.

6. Serve cheesecakes warm, on a pool of sauce.

Makes 4 servings.

Per serving: calories 615; protein 8.2 g; fat 30 g; carbohydrate 78 g; sodium 352 mg

Thaw phyllo in refrigerator overnight. Sauce can be made day ahead. Refrigerate.

A Thai Getaway

The first thing you should know about Thai food in general, and this meal in particular, is that you won't be using chopsticks. Get out the spoons and forks instead, and don't be afraid to use your fingers! (Not knives – they symbolize aggression). The second thing to remember about Thai cooking is that it only has to be as hot as you want it to be.

More aromatic from herbs than spices, Thai cuisine has been shaped by the cooking of China, India, Japan and the Middle East, as peoples from all these countries have settled into the region at various times during its past 27,000 years. And each culture has left its imprint. Contemporary Thai cuisine engages the taste buds in an artful interplay of sweet, salty, sour and spicy flavours; the finesse with which it does so is largely a legacy of royal cooks from a century ago. Typical Thai seasonings include lime, chili peppers, coriander, lemon grass and the aromatic ginger called galangal. Coconut milk is another one of those indispensable ingredients. It's to Thai cooks what cream is to French chefs, an essential cooking liquid.

Thai food is easy-going yet sophisticated, and that's how your dinner experience should be. Don't doubt your ability to tackle this exotic menu, thinking, "I wish I were a better cook." If that's your mantra, you'll love how quickly this dinner comes together, and how minimal the real hands-on work.

Just think: In the old days, a Thai curry made from scratch often required the better part of the cook's morning. That's how much time was given over to pounding the herbs and spices that give it such depths of flavour!

Menu for 4

PC *Frozen Black Tiger Shrimp in Crisp Wrappers*

Mussels in Green Curry Sauce

PC *Frozen Thai Noodles with Coconut Chicken*

Jasmine Rice Balls

Mango Sherbet with Fruit

The wine – full-bodied fruity white *gewurztraminer or dry muscat*

Allow 1 hour. Prepare rice balls; refrigerate. Heat **PC** *Thai noodle dish in microwave. Bake* **PC** *shrimp appetizers. Prepare mussels. Prepare dessert.*

Mussels in Green Curry Sauce

The coconut milk in the curry sauce adds flavour and tames the spices.

1 can (284 mL)	*PC* Thai Green Curry Sauce (see Note)
1 lb (500 g)	live mussels
1/2 cup (125 mL)	finely diced sweet red pepper
1/2 cup (125 mL)	chopped fresh coriander

1. In large saucepan, bring Thai sauce to a boil. Add mussels; cover and cook over high heat for 3 to 5 minutes or until mussels have opened. Discard any that do not open.

2. Remove pan from heat. Stir in red pepper and coriander. Transfer to large serving platter. Serve with rice balls.

Makes 4 servings.

Note: For a spicier dish, substitute *PC* Thai Yellow Curry Sauce.

Per serving: calories 173; protein 9.4 g; fat 11 g; carbohydrate 9.1 g; sodium 568 mg

PC Frozen Black Tiger Shrimp in Crisp Wrappers (pictured)

*A popular hors d'oeuvre on Thai menus, these shrimp have a mild Asian seasoning and are wrapped in crisp pastry that's reminiscent of spring-roll wrappers. For dipping, put out a small bowl of **PC Memories of** Thailand Fiery Thai Dipping Sauce, as shown here, or **PC Memories of** Canton Hot Plum Sauce.*

PC Frozen Thai Noodles with Coconut Chicken

A rich-tasting, Alfredo-like dish but Thai-style – the egg noodles, seasoned chicken breast pieces, and vegetables are all tossed in a creamy coconut sauce flavoured with lemon grass, Kaffir lime and chili.

Jasmine Rice Balls

Slightly sticky jasmine rice has a light flowery taste.

1 3/4 cups (425 mL)	water
1 cup (250 mL)	*PC* Jasmine Thai Rice, rinsed
1/4 cup (50 mL)	chopped fresh coriander

1. In small saucepan, bring water to a boil. Add rice; cover and cook over low heat for 8 to 10 minutes or until water is absorbed. Cool for 10 minutes. Stir in coriander.

2. Wet hands with cold water. Place 2 tbsp (25 mL) of cooled rice mixture into palm of one hand. Use other hand to shape rice into a ball. Place on platter. Repeat with remaining rice. Serve at room temperature with mussels.

Makes 4 servings.

Per serving: calories 179; protein 3.5 g; fat 0.5 g; carbohydrate 40 g; sodium 6.7 mg

Mango Sherbet with Fruit

Talented Thai cooks can carve tropical fruits into works of art.

8 scoops	*PC* Mango Sherbet
2	fresh mangoes, peeled and sliced
2 cups (500 mL)	fresh strawberries, sliced
	Mint sprigs

1. Place two scoops of sherbet into each of four dessert dishes. Arrange sliced mango and strawberries around sherbet. Garnish with mint.

Makes 4 servings.

Per serving: calories 234; protein 1.4 g; fat 1.4 g; carbohydrate 54 g; sodium 22 mg

A Hearty Vegetarian Feast

The Portuguese have a saying, "He who looks at faces doesn't see the heart" (*Quem ve cara não ve coração*), which is used in many situations to encourage people to look beyond appearances to see what matters. It could even apply to this novel menu because while satisfying, it contains no meat whatsoever. What's a hungry body to do if it's accustomed to having its meat and potatoes?

Fret not, for there is ample nourishment here and more than enough flavour excitement for eight lucky people. It's *la grande bouffe*, vegetarian-style. Ask your teenaged son or daughter to fill you in on all the reasons it helps to go meatless, if not every day, then on occasion, and especially when there's a good reason for doing so. This menu is a very good reason. (Let them help you prepare it. You're already off the hook

for the French-style vegetable stew, ratatouille, and the fruit dessert.)

Cooks who are attracted by the recipes offered here, but are wondering if meatless dishes are suitable fare for company ("Won't they miss the roast?") should be encouraged by the great gourmet food revelation of our day: Vegetable-based cooking is inherently fun and always interesting. In the Old World, people learned to be creative in using what was at hand, for it was rarely meat. It was more often beans, grains and dairy products. The smooth white bean soup and rustic looking Spinach-Rice Phyllo Pie, for example, are both inspired by the peasant cooking of Europe, the kind of tasty, substantial fare that's now called budget gourmet. So dig in – nobody goes away hungry from this table.

Menu for 8

Vegetable Patty Dip

White Bean and Garlic Soup with Sourdough Croutons

Spinach-Rice Phyllo Pie

Roasted Stuffed Portobello Mushrooms

PC Too Good To Be True
Frozen Ratatouille

PC Frozen Berry-Cherry Crisp with
PC Vanilla Decadence *Ice Cream*

The wine – herbal white
New Zealand or Chilean sauvignon blanc

Thaw spinach and phyllo in refrigerator overnight. Allow 3 hours for meal. Make dip; refrigerate. Bake pie. Purée soup; set aside. 15 minutes before pie comes out, put mushrooms in to bake. Heat ratatouille in microwave. Reheat soup. Bake crisp.

Spinach-Rice Phyllo Pie

A delicious and stunning buffet centrepiece that's easier to assemble than it looks.

1 cup (250 mL)	raw *PC* White Basmati Rice, freshly cooked according to package instructions and cooled
1 tbsp (15 mL)	grated lemon rind
2 tbsp (25 mL)	fresh lemon juice
1	egg
1 pkg (340 g)	*PC Splendido* Partly Skimmed Stretched Mozzarella Cheese (approx. 3 cups/750 mL), shredded
	Salt and freshly ground black pepper
2 pkg (each 300 g)	frozen chopped spinach, thawed and squeezed dry
1 tsp (5 mL)	*PC* Chopped Garlic in Oil
1/2 tsp (2 mL)	ground nutmeg
	PC Too Good To Be True The Virtuous Vegetable Oil Cooking Spray, butter flavoured
6 sheets	*PC* Frozen Phyllo, thawed
2 cups (500 mL)	*PC* 7-Vegetable Primavera Pasta Sauce

1. Preheat oven to 375°F (190°C).
2. In large bowl, stir together cooked cooled rice, lemon rind and juice, egg, 1 1/2 cups (375 mL) of the cheese and pinch each of salt and pepper.
3. In another bowl, combine spinach, garlic, nutmeg, remaining cheese and pinch each of salt and pepper.
4. Spray 9-inch (23 cm) pie plate with cooking spray. Place one sheet of phyllo over left side of pie plate, pressing into bottom and letting it overlap sides of plate. Spray with cooking spray. Place another sheet over right side of pie plate in the same manner, slightly overlapping first sheet. Repeat with remaining phyllo sheets, alternately placing the sheets to the left and to the right, overlapping them and spraying each with cooking spray.
5. Spread half of the rice mixture over bottom of pie plate. Top with half of the spinach mixture. Pour half of the pasta sauce over spinach layer. Repeat layers. Bring hanging edges of phyllo up and over filling, crumpling slightly. Spray top with cooking spray.
6. Bake for 30 minutes. Cover loosely with foil. Bake another 45 minutes. Let stand for 10 minutes before slicing.

Makes 8 servings.

Per serving: calories 338; protein 19 g; fat 10 g; carbohydrate 43 g; sodium 803 mg
Pie may be assembled the day before baking. Refrigerate. Add 10 minutes to covered baking time.

Roasted Stuffed Portobello Mushrooms

The meaty texture of portobellos makes this dish suitable for light meals too.

8	portobello mushrooms
6	*PC* Swedish Crisp Toasts
Half	a 350 g pkg *PC Too Good To Be True* Extra Firm Herb Tofu
3	green onions, thinly sliced
1/3 cup (75 mL)	*PC* Golden Sesame Oriental Vinaigrette
1/2 cup (125 mL)	*PC* Raisin-Cranberry Portage Mix
1 tbsp (15 mL)	finely chopped fresh thyme
1/2 tsp (2 mL) each	salt and freshly ground black pepper

1. Preheat oven to 375°F (190°C).

2. Remove stems from mushrooms. Wipe mushroom caps clean. Spray both sides of mushroom caps with butter-flavoured cooking spray. Arrange gill side down on rimmed baking sheet. Bake for 10 minutes.

3. Meanwhile, in food processor, crush toasts to make crumbs. Place in bowl. Crumble tofu into bowl. Stir in green onions, vinaigrette, Portage Mix, thyme, salt and pepper.

4. Remove mushrooms from oven. Turn mushrooms over. Divide tofu mixture among caps, mounding slightly. Return to oven. Bake 15 minutes longer.

Makes 8 servings.

Per serving: calories 186; protein 8.6 g; fat 10 g; carbohydrate 15 g; sodium 281 mg

PC Too Good To Be True
Frozen Ratatouille

A mixed vegetable stew made with tomatoes, onions and eggplant is one of the traditional foods of the South of France.

Vegetable Patty Dip

This hearty, full-flavoured dip can double as a sandwich filling.

4	*PC Too Good To Be True* Frozen Ancient Grains Vegetable Patties
1/2 cup (125 mL)	*PC* Light Mayonnaise Type Dressing
4	green onions, thinly sliced
	Assorted *PC TGTBT* Crackers

1. Preheat oven to 425°F (220°C). Spray both sides of patties with cooking spray. Place patties on baking sheet. Bake for 15 minutes. Transfer patties to bowl. Using a fork, mash patties. Let cool for 10 minutes.

2. Stir in dressing and green onions. Transfer to serving bowl. Refrigerate. Serve with crackers. Makes about 2 cups (500 mL).

Makes 8 servings, about 1/4 cup (50 mL) each.

Per serving of dip: calories 135; protein 2.8 g; fat 6.2 g; carbohydrate 17 g; sodium 155 mg

White Bean and Garlic Soup with Sourdough Croutons

A smooth-textured soup with the sweetness of white beans and a hint of rosemary.

1 tbsp (15 mL)	*PC Splendido* Extra Virgin Olive Oil
2 cups (500 mL)	coarsely chopped onions
3 cups (750 mL)	homemade vegetable stock (or from bouillon cube)
1 bottle (796 mL)	*PC Too Good To Be True* Great Northern Beans, undrained
1/2 cup (125 mL)	*PC Memories of Gilroy* Creamy Roasted Garlic Sauce & Dressing
	Salt and freshly ground black pepper
1 cup (250 mL)	*PC* Ranch Flavour Sourdough Croutons
2 tsp (10 mL)	chopped fresh rosemary

1. In saucepan, heat oil over medium heat; cook onions for 5 minutes or until tender. Transfer to blender or food processor along with 1 cup (250 mL) of the stock. Purée. Return mixture to saucepan.

2. In batches, purée beans with remaining stock, and add to onion mixture. Stir in *Memories of Gilroy*. Cook over medium heat for 10 minutes or until hot. Season to taste with salt and pepper. Serve garnished with croutons and rosemary.

Makes 8 servings.

Per serving: calories 234; protein 7.9 g; fat 11.2 g; carbohydrate 26 g; sodium 647 mg

PC Frozen Berry-Cherry Crisp with PC Vanilla Decadence Ice Cream

Cranberries, blackberries, blueberries and cherries come together in a mixed berry crisp with a crunchy oatmeal topping. Served warm out of the oven...à la mode, of course.

The Cheese Tray

Every cheese is a new experience. It has as much to do with how it spends its formative days as it does with the milk from which it was made. Was it set to rest in the chill moisture of a mould-rich mountain cave? Or was it tended and turned in a cool, dry cellar? Perhaps the cheese matured in a draughty attic. Many diverse environments, including the carefully controlled conditions under which commercial cheeses are made, are places where cheeses develop flavour, aided by friendly organisms that help coax wobbly white curd into rewarding eating. From its first milky moments, Nature is in charge.

Cheese is a cultured product. It can be made quickly to be eaten quickly, like cottage cheese, or aged like Cheddar for longer keeping. It's almost impossible to believe that all cheeses start off the same way, from clabber...softly curdled milk that gives off a sweet lactic aroma. The future of a cheese will be determined by the size of the curds, whether they're cooked or not, whether drained or pressed, how salted and when, and by which micro-organisms are called on to give them flavour. Even its size as it ripens helps determine the future of a cheese. Brick and Limburger, for instance, are very close cousins. But where Brick matures in a big block, Limburger is cut into small, thin, rectangular slabs to speed ripening throughout the cheese, giving it a completely different flavour and aroma, and making it very creamy.

The cheese tray is where you get an opportunity to taste the results of a cheesemaker's many decisions.

Cultures are born and die, but cheese is immortal.

Icelandic saying

Cheese has been in the making since about 6000 BC. It was put in the tombs of the pharaohs to sustain them on their journey to the land of the dead. When Little Miss Muffet of latter-day fame sat down on her tuffet, it was to enjoy curds and whey – the point at which milk makes its "leap to immortality" and begins to turn into cheese. With the whey drained off, cheese has a beginning. Cottage cheese is soft fresh curd. That makes it bland compared to cheeses which are allowed to dehydrate so that their flavour becomes concentrated, as in Parmigiano Reggiano, which was officially recognized as a distinct make of cheese in 1579.

The natural flora of the milk greatly enhances the flavour of unpasteurized milk cheeses, whether the milk itself comes from cow, goat, sheep or buffalo. You can be sure that cheese made from hay-fed cows tastes distinctly different than if they grazed on herb-rich pastures. Cheese made from pasteurized milk receives harmless cultures for its flavour development and texture. These organisms may work from the outside in, as on a surface-ripened cheese like Brie, or from the inside out, as in the case of a Swiss-type cheese where pockets of gas cause "eyes." To make blue cheese, unpressed white cheese is introduced to a grayish-green mould that eventually works its way into the interior through holes pierced in the cheese.

For the love of cheese

When Nadine Ridel of La Ferme, in Pefferlaw, Ontario, purveyors of foie gras to the restaurant trade, wants to treat herself, she takes some bread, red wine and cheese – the three elements some call the "holy trinity" of the table. "It's very personal. You eat the cheese you like," says Mme Ridel, who grew up eating Camembert in Normandy, France, but is particularly fond of St. Marcellin. "At dinner, it's always after the entrée and salad, and you leave room for dessert. In restaurants in France, they have a cheese trolley and you say, 'I want a piece of Camembert and a piece of chèvre, I want to try a little bit of Roquefort, not too much...' and you end up with a little display on your plate."

Each type of cheese has its own personality. The rind may be downy-soft and the inside unctuous, as in a Brillat Savarin. Its flavour may be bland or sharp, or fruity or nutty. (The flavour of hazelnut in Gruyere actually arises from the same flavour compounds found in hazelnuts themselves.) Let the chart on page 92 be your guide.

Cheese...At Its Most Inviting

A wooden board is convenient because it's easy to cut on. Or use a pretty platter or a wicker tray, which permits ventilation (but not marble – it makes cheese sweat). Give blue cheese its own knife. Return cheeses to room temperature at least one hour before serving and longer for some Bries and Camembert. (Ask for advice when buying.) Cover the cheese tray loosely with a clean tea towel to allow the cheeses to breathe.

Add fruit or not. (Fresh figs can be delicious.) "Generally, in France, when we eat cheese, we eat cheese," says Nadine Ridel. "I would rather put different breads on the platter, such as a walnut bread. It goes well with cheese. That's my personal taste. I like dark rye with a Camembert or a creamy cheese. All types of bread can work, and there is such a good selection today."

Bread also comes in handy for cleaning the cheese knife between uses, to avoid mixing flavours. Biscuits should not be too salty. Whole grain crackers work well with blue cheeses. You can put out some butter for firm, dry cheeses.

Pictured from left:
PC 2-Year-Old White
Canadian Cheddar Cheese,
PC Herbed Goat's Milk
Cheese, President French
Emmental, Stilton, Canadian
Double-Cream Brie.
Front: Parmigiano Reggiano.

Texture	Flavours	Cheeses
SOFT (creamy, succulent)	aromatic	French or Canadian Brie, Camembert
SEMI-SOFT (sliceable)	tangy, yeasty	medium Canadian Oka, Havarti, goat's milk mozzarella
	buttery	Canadian Tome
	barnyardy	German Munster
	salty	feta
	pungent	French Chaume
	aromatic	Italian Taleggio
FIRM (sliceable)	nutty-sweet	Dutch Edam, Swiss-type cheeses
	mild	Gouda, Cheddar
	earthy	Gruyere
HARD (crumbly)	tangy	old Cheddar
	sharp	extra old Cheddar, aged Gouda
	nutty	Parmigiano Reggiano, aged Spanish Manchego
BLUE (creamy to crumbly)	pungent	Italian Gorgonzola
	tangy, intense	Roquefort, Stilton, Danish blue

Buying cheese

"A 100 g to 130 g piece is the start of a decent cut of cheese," says Nadine Ridel, pointing out that some cheeses must be purchased intact. "If you organize a party just with cheese, you will need a lot because people will rush to the cheese table and take big bites. So if it is cheese alone, you will need about one kilogram (2.2 lb) for six to 12 people.

"If you want to buy cheese for a party, you will buy it ripe for that day so everyone enjoys it. Buy your cheese slightly underripe if you intend to eat it over a few days or a week and not in one sitting. It will continue to ripen in your fridge. We always try to have cheese that's ready to eat."

Ask your cheese seller for advice. And let touch guide you when determining if a surface-ripened cheese like Brie is ready to eat; it should spring back when gently pressed. A strong smell of ammonia in a Brie is the sign of over-ripeness. You might catch a whiff of it when you remove the wrapper from packaged cheese (gases come naturally to cheese), but the scent should dissipate immediately.

Putting the tray together

You can't go wrong if you remember to:
- buy what you like
- buy cheese that is already ripe
- buy different textured cheese
- find a cheese purveyor that you can trust.

Look close to home for some fine cheeses. Much of the world's best Cheddar is made right here in Canada (look for Royal Winter Fair prize-winners). And Canada topped the Brie category at the 2000 World Championship Cheese Contest with an Ontario Brie. Quebec's Oka originated with Trappist monks in 1893. Some Ontario cheeses are now being made exclusively from the rich milk of Jersey cows, one of the world's oldest dairy breeds. (Jersey cows are tan-coloured with pretty faces – the ones that owners like to give names such as Buttercup or Regina.)

Also keep on the lookout for variations on favourite cheeses. Tuxford & Tebbut's Five Counties Cheese from Britain, for example, is a black-waxed cheese made with separate layers of five different Cheddars. Be adventurous. Try a traditional, name-protected cheese from France. Some can be real 'stinkers' but they offer flavour excitement. British Wensleydale, a cow's milk cheese, is traditionally eaten with fruitcake. Stilton with port, of course, is a classic for year-end celebrations. Also, visit cheese specialty shops for an education in exotic and hard-to-find cheeses. There may be one from Spain or Greece that will be to your liking.

As a guide, choose five cheeses from the chart on page 92, selecting one from each category. For two people, three cheeses should do, and might include a goat cheese from Ontario (PC Herbed or Peppercorn Goat's Milk Cheese) or one surface-ripened semi-soft cheese (Tournevant from Quebec); one "nutty" cheese (Jersey Farms Edam from Ontario, or French-made Emmental); and one stronger cheese (aged Cheddar or for 'blue' lovers, a rich Stilton, England's only name-protected cheese.)

When cutting a piece of cheese, or when helping yourself to some from the tray, be sure to take a piece of the rind. The cheese tends to be riper there, and will yield a different flavour.

Don't stop at wine to enjoy with your cheese. Try Champagne. Or beer – light beer with Jalapeño Monterey Jack, lager with Friulano, or stout with old Provolone (put some salami and olives on the plate for an Italian-style antipasto).

Keeping cheese

"Unless you are really a connoisseur, you will put the cheese in the fridge with everything else," says Mme Ridel. "Keep your cheese well-wrapped, preferably in its original container, in the vegetable bin of the refrigerator. I leave it in the wrapper or in the box because they already have a special coating. We try to remember to take it out before dinner because there is nothing more unpleasant to eat than a very cold cheese."

Cheese cannot withstand numerous temperature changes, so remove only what you will manage to eat. Cheddar and Swiss-type cheeses can keep for several weeks if well-wrapped in plastic. Wrap Parmigiano Reggiano in a double thickness of aluminum foil. If it starts to dry out (the colour will whiten), wrap it in a piece of moist cheesecloth, then overwrap it with foil and leave it overnight. Next day, remove the cheesecloth and rewrap the cheese. (By the way, when you get down to the rind, don't throw it away; toss it into a vegetable soup for flavour.)

A Thanksgiving Buffet

Thanksgiving isn't a normal day. One look in the dining room confirms this, for what you have here is a veritable picture of abundance. The table is a groaning board of temptations, weighted down with everyone's favourite dishes. Sideboards must be brought into service on this occasion to hold the overflow of sweet and savoury delights.

Since most people love the comfort foods they grew up with, in many families the highlight of this meal is a golden, roasted turkey. In the wild, the turkey is often mistaken for guinea hen. Actually, it's a variety of pheasant. Christopher Columbus assumed the toms he saw strutting about, gobbling to draw hens near and making a sound that people liken to an 18-wheeler shifting into gear, were some kind of New World peacock.

Thinking he was still on land that was connected to India, he called them *tuka*, the Indian name for peacock. That early association is reflected in the French *dinde* (d'inde, or "of India") and the Italian *pavone d'India* (Indian rooster). The colonies shipped boatloads of wild turkeys back to France in the early 1800s, even though they cost the French people almost as much as truffles.

We love the smell of turkey roasting, but finding other things to gobble up with it can pose a problem. Since Thanksgiving falls at a time of year when one has all the flavours of the harvest to draw on, that's what we did. For food safety reasons, we recommend cooking a stuffing separately from the turkey. Also, an unstuffed turkey cooks more quickly, meaning that you and your family will be able to dig in faster.

Menu for 8

Pâté and Cheese Tray

Roast Turkey

Sage & Onion Wedges

Roasted Garlic-Scented Root Vegetables

Dilled Beet Gratin

Kale and Cabbage Salad

Apple Crunch Pie

The wine – light oaked red *pinot noir*
For dessert – *Canadian icewine*

Thaw turkey (see p. 24) in refrigerator 3 days. Allow 5 1/2 hours for meal. Make wedges. Assemble gratin (refrigerate unbaked). Put turkey in oven. Assemble pie (do not bake). Remove turkey. Bake gratin and vegetables. Assemble tray. Make salad. Bake pie.

Roast Turkey

Use the giblets and neck from the turkey to make stock for your favourite gravy recipe.

1	*PC* Frozen Butter Basted Turkey with Giblets (12 to 14 lb/5.4 to 6.4 kg), thawed

1. Preheat oven to 325°F (160°C).
2. Remove giblets and neck from turkey. Do not stuff turkey. Place turkey in large roasting pan. Roast uncovered for 3 1/4 to 4 hours, or until meat thermometer reads 185°F (85°C) at thickest part of thigh.
3. Transfer turkey to serving platter. Tent loosely with foil. Let stand 20 minutes before carving.

Makes 8 servings, with generous leftovers.

Per 6 oz/175 g serving: calories 299; protein 32 g; fat 19 g; carbohydrate 0 g; sodium 109 mg

Kale and Cabbage Salad

Grainy prepared mustard imparts a gentle flavour to the apple cider dressing.

4 cups (1 L)	kale, torn into bite-sized pieces (about 1 bunch)
4 cups (1 L)	finely sliced Chinese (Napa) cabbage
4 strips	*PC* Fully Cooked Bacon, diced
1	Granny Smith apple, diced (not peeled)
1/2 cup (125 mL)	*PC* Light Mayonnaise Type Dressing
1/2 cup (125 mL)	*PC* Fresh Pressed Sweet Apple Cider
1 tsp (5 mL)	*PC* Old-Fashioned Whole Grain Dijon Prepared Mustard

1. In large bowl, combine kale, cabbage, bacon and apple.
2. In small bowl, whisk together mayonnaise, cider and mustard.
3. Pour dressing over salad; toss to coat.

Makes 8 servings.

Per serving: calories 105; protein 2.6 g; fat 6.2 g; carbohydrate 38 g; sodium 54 mg

Dilled Beet Gratin

Bunch beets have a less earthy flavour than storage beets.

2 lb (1 kg)	beets (6 to 8 medium)
1/2 cup (125 mL)	chopped fresh dill
1 tbsp (15 mL)	grated lemon rind
1 pkg (140 g)	*PC* Ranch Flavour Sourdough Croutons, lightly crushed
1/2 cup (125 mL)	*PC Memories of* Reggiano Parmigiano-Reggiano Caesar Dressing
3/4 cup (175 mL)	10% cream
1/4 tsp (1 mL) each	salt and freshly ground black pepper

1. Add beets to large pot of cold, salted water. Bring to a boil. Reduce heat to medium, cover and cook until tender when pierced with the tip of a knife, about 30 to 45 minutes. Drain. Place under cold running water until cool enough to handle. Slip off skins. Slice 1/4 inch (0.5 cm) thick.

2. Preheat oven to 375°F (190°C).

3. In small bowl, mix together dill and lemon rind.

4. Scatter half of beets over bottom of 13-by-9-inch (3.5 L) baking dish. Sprinkle with dill mixture, then 1/2 cup (125 mL) of croutons. Top with remaining beets.

5. In bowl, whisk together dressing, cream, salt and pepper. Pour over beet mixture. Sprinkle with remaining croutons. Bake, uncovered, for 30 minutes.

Makes 8 servings.

Per serving: calories 299; protein 4.9 g; fat 15 g; carbohydrate 19 g; sodium 461 mg

Sage and Onion Wedges

All the flavours of turkey stuffing in moist, scone-like wedges.
Perfect for soaking up gravy and for making turkey sandwiches.

10 strips	*PC* Fully Cooked Bacon, chopped
3 cups (750 mL)	*PC* Uncommonly Light Biscuit Mix
1 cup (250 mL)	chopped celery
1 cup (250 mL)	chopped onions
1/4 cup (50 mL)	finely chopped fresh sage
1/4 tsp (1 mL) each	salt and freshly ground black pepper
3/4 cup (175 mL)	milk

1. Position rack in centre of oven and preheat to 400°F (200°C). Spray 10-inch (3 L) springform pan with cooking spray.

2. In bowl, stir together bacon, biscuit mix, celery, onions, sage, salt and pepper. Stir in milk until mixture holds together. Gently press mixture into prepared pan. Score top into 8 wedges.

3. Bake for 40 to 45 minutes. Serve warm or at room temperature.

Makes 8 servings.

Per serving: calories 225; protein 6.6 g; fat 9.6 g; carbohydrate 28 g; sodium 822 mg

Roasted Garlic-Scented Root Vegetables

With this treatment, even parsnips are as easy to eat as candy.

1 lb (500 g)	parsnips, peeled
1 lb (500 g)	carrots, peeled
2 lb (1 kg)	baking potatoes, peeled
1/4 cup (50 mL)	*PC* Roasted Garlic Flavoured Olive Oil
1/4 tsp (1 mL) each	salt and freshly ground black pepper

1. Preheat oven to 375 F (190 C).
2. Cut vegetables into 1 1/2 inch (4 cm) pieces. Add to large pot of boiling, salted water and cook for 10 minutes. Drain.
3. Toss vegetables with garlic oil, salt and pepper. Spread over large rimmed baking sheet. Bake for 30 minutes or until tender.
4. Transfer to serving platter.

Makes 8 servings.

Per serving: calories 224; protein 3.7 g; fat 7.2 g; carbohydrate 36 g; sodium 106 mg

Vegetables can be prepared night before. Do not parboil. Toss with garlic oil, salt and pepper. Roast 30 minutes at 375°F (190°C). Cool. Cover and refrigerate overnight. Next day, return to oven after removing turkey. Cook 15 to 20 minutes or until golden brown.

Pâté and Cheese Tray

A pleasant addition to the meal. Pictured above, from left:

PC Rustic Peppercorn Pâté
PC 2-Year-Old White Canadian Cheddar Cheese
PC 1-Year-Old Marble Cheddar Cheese
PC Ardennes-Style Pâté
PC Biscuits for Cheese

Apple Crunch Pie

*The key to this delectable creation is making sure the
PC Apple Pie is completely defrosted before you begin.
Give it a good night in the refrigerator.*

1/4 cup (50 mL)	*PC* Fresh Churned Unsalted Butter
1/2 cup (125 mL)	packed brown sugar
1/4 cup (50 mL)	all-purpose flour
2 tsp (10 mL)	cinnamon
2 cups (500 mL)	*PC* Low Fat Raisin & Almond Granola Clusters
1	*PC* Frozen Apple Pie, fully thawed
1 tbsp (15 mL)	milk
2 tbsp (25 mL)	granulated sugar

1. Place butter in freezer for 30 minutes. Position rack in centre of oven and preheat to 400°F (200°C).

2. In bowl, combine brown sugar, flour and cinnamon. Grate butter into bowl; toss with flour mixture. Add granola; toss to combine.

3. Keep pie in foil pie plate. Place pie on baking sheet. With sharp knife, make a large X in the centre of the top crust to within 1 inch (2.5 cm) of edge of pie. Fold back crust. Pack granola mixture onto exposed apple filling. Fold crust back over granola mixture. (If pastry cracks, gently press back into place.)

4. Brush milk all over pie crust. Sprinkle with sugar. Bake for 20 minutes. Loosely cover with foil. Bake another 40 minutes. Serve warm.

Makes 8 servings.

Per serving: calories 555; protein 6.2 g; fat 22 g; carbohydrate 83 g; sodium 371 mg

A Cozy Fireside Supper

The way to approach winter is like a child, an agreeable child. A child is little preoccupied with thoughts that belong in a grown-up's head – like how disruptive a snowfall is going to be for driving. Why worry about it? Life intends to keep you busy, even in winter, when there are so many fun activities to do that you can't do any other time of year. And a day like today holds such promise.

From the moment you open the door, you step into a winter wonderland. The morning is aglow. Ahead, the sun is rising warm and rose-coloured. It throws its fetching pastel tint across the sky like a wash of colour; it suffuses your cheeks, to anyone who is watching. A sun like any other day, but not quite the same, ever. Good thing it's still early enough to make plans for an outing. What will it be? Skiing? Tobogganing? Ice skating? Even a walk through the snowy drifts when the air is chill and crisp can do wonders for family and friends. Later, when you're all famished, you can sit down to eat in front of the fireplace.

All it takes to bring this cozy menu together is a well-stocked pantry and freezer, and a few vegetables from the late-fall harvest in your cold storage. Check these recipes for make-ahead tips, for you can put much of the dinner together ahead of time, in bits and pieces. The few last-minute touches needed can wait until you're all back home, cheeks flushed and rosy. If there are children in the picture, that's fine. They won't have to tiptoe around this dinner, trying not to make any sudden noises that might ruin the cook's concentration. It's not that kind of meal. Get them to help you decorate the dessert. It's what little hands like to get themselves into...

Menu for 4

*Roasted Butternut Squash Soup
with Butter-Crusted Beer Bread*

PC Frozen Fireside Pie

Cabbage and Bacon Slaw

Rich Hot Mint Chocolate

Chocolate Vanilla Cookie Cheesecake

*The wine – a full mellow red
Australian shiraz or
Canadian baco noir*

*Allow 3 1/2 hours. Bake bread. Bake squash
for soup. Prepare cheesecake; refrigerate.
Make soup to point of puréeing; cover and
set off heat. Bake Fireside Pie. Make slaw.
Reheat soup. Make hot chocolate.*

PC Frozen Fireside Pie

Inspired by shepherd's pie, the original meat-and-potatoes entrée, this tasty variation has a rich filling made with ground beef and vegetables, and comes with a layer of cheesy potato topping. Simply reheat in the oven or microwave.

Cabbage and Bacon Slaw

Savoy cabbage, a crinkly variety, has less of a bite than green cabbage.

7 slices	*PC* Fully Cooked Bacon (half a 65 g pkg)
3 cups (750 mL)	thinly sliced Savoy cabbage
3 cups (750 mL)	thinly sliced red cabbage
1/2 cup (125 mL)	*PC* Fat Free Honey Dijon Dressing

1. Cook bacon in microwave oven for 25 seconds on High to crisp. Chop.
2. In large serving bowl, combine Savoy cabbage, red cabbage, and bacon.
3. Pour dressing over; toss to coat.

Makes 6 servings.

Per serving: calories 94; protein 2.9 g; fat 2.5 g; carbohydrate 15 g; sodium 254 mg

Roasted Butternut Squash Soup

A silken-textured soup with the colour of the harvest moon.

1	large butternut squash (2 lb/1 kg)
1 tbsp (15 mL)	PC Fresh Concentrated Chicken Stock
3 cups (750 mL)	boiling water
1 tbsp (15 mL)	butter
1 cup (250 mL)	chopped onions
1 tbsp (15 mL)	fresh lemon juice
1/4 tsp (1 mL)	ground nutmeg
	Salt and freshly ground black pepper
1 tbsp (15 mL)	chopped fresh parsley

1. Preheat oven to 400°F (200°C).
2. Cut squash in half lengthwise. Scoop out seeds. Place cut side down on large rimmed baking sheet. Bake for 40 to 50 minutes or until tender when pierced with a skewer. Cool.
3. Dissolve chicken stock concentrate in boiling water.
4. In large saucepan, melt butter over medium heat; cook onions for 5 minutes or until tender.
5. Scoop flesh from cooled squash and transfer to blender or food processor. Add onion mixture and 1 cup (250 mL) of the stock; purée, adding more stock as necessary. Return mixture to saucepan along with any remaining stock.
6. Cook over medium heat for 10 minutes or until heated through. Stir in lemon juice and nutmeg. Season to taste with salt and pepper. Serve garnished with parsley.

Makes 4 servings.

Per serving: calories 123; protein 2.2 g; fat 3.8 g; carbohydrate 20 g; sodium 355 mg

Soup can be made early in day. After puréeing, refrigerate. Reheat before serving.

Butter-Crusted Beer Bread

You won't taste the beer, just the buttery crispness of the crust.

2 1/2 cups (625 mL)	self-rising flour
1/4 cup (50 mL)	chopped fresh parsley
2 tbsp (25 mL)	granulated sugar
1 bottle (341 mL)	PC Draft Beer
1/4 cup (50 mL)	PC Fresh Churned Salted Butter, melted

1. Position rack in centre of oven and preheat to 350°F (180°C). Spray 9-by-5-inch (2 L) loaf pan with cooking spray.
2. In standing mixer using paddle attachment, mix flour, parsley and sugar on low speed for 1 minute. Add beer; continue to mix on low speed for 1 minute longer or until beer is thoroughly incorporated. (Alternatively, mix ingredients in large bowl with wooden spoon.)
3. Pour batter into prepared loaf pan. Pour melted butter on top. Place pan on baking sheet. Bake for 45 to 55 minutes or until tester inserted in centre comes out clean. Let stand for 10 minutes before serving.

Makes 1 loaf (12 slices).

Per slice: calories 138; protein 2.7 g; fat 4.3 g; carbohydrate 22 g; sodium 362 mg

Can be made day ahead. Do not refrigerate. Wrap with plastic wrap or waxed paper and store at room temperature.

Chocolate Vanilla Cookie Cheesecake

Ask the children to help you with this super easy dessert.

| 1 pkg (650 g) | PC Frozen Original New York Style Cheesecake |
| 10 | PC 'Eat the Middle First!' Chocolate Vanilla Creme Cookies |

1. Place cheesecake on serving dish. Let stand at room temperature for 30 minutes.
2. Using serrated knife, gently cut 5 cookies in half. Place cookie semi-circles standing up on top of cheesecake around outside edge.
3. Place remaining 5 cookies in food processor; process for 30 seconds or until reduced to coarse crumbs. (Alternatively, place cookies in plastic bag and coarsely crush.) Sprinkle half of the cookie crumbs over top of cake. Press remaining cookie crumbs around sides of cake. Refrigerate.
4. Remove from refrigerator 30 minutes before serving.

Makes 6 servings.

Per serving: calories 442; protein 7.9 g; fat 30 g; carbohydrate 35 g; sodium 331 mg

Rich Hot Mint Chocolate

Extra minty and luxurious from chocolate mint candies.

3/4 cup (175 mL)	PC Extra-Rich Chocolate Flavour Instant Hot Chocolate
3 cups (750 mL)	boiling water
4	PC Mint Miniatures
1/2 cup (125 mL)	whipping cream (optional)

1. Place about 3 tbsp (45 mL) instant hot chocolate into each of four mugs. Stir in boiling water. Add one mint miniature to each mug; stir until chocolate is melted.
2. In bowl, whip cream, if using. Divide whipped cream among mugs and serve.

Makes 4 servings.

Per serving: calories 225; protein 3.6 g; fat 11 g; carbohydrate 27 g; sodium 157 mg
Per serving without whipped cream: calories 178; protein 3.3 g; fat 6.3 g; carbohydrate 27 g; sodium 152 mg

A Warming Provençal Meal

The season has settled in hard, like a stiff wool blanket. Daylight is so thin, and it ekes out to darkness so quickly. You need more than a summer memory now to sustain you. A comforting stew to top off the day should help lift the spirits. The substantial fare we have in mind on this particular occasion is hearty Provençal-style braised beef, with the distinctive herbal perfume that only fresh thyme can impart.

Occupying the south-east corner of France between the Rhone River and the Italian Alps, Provence is dotted with medieval hill towns and blessed with the Mediterranean lapping at its front steps. Foods borne of this landscape appeal directly to the senses. The flavour of the place is lusty, yet the cooking is simplicity itself. While the magic of Provençal food is how it manages to be cooling on hot days, a warming menu featuring its characteristic flavours feels most appropriate when the air is frigid.

Our beef daube begins and ends by putting everything in a covered casserole – a modern variation of the three-legged covered pot that used to be pushed deep into the fireplace coals in the French farmhouse kitchen. In Provence, it is customary to serve daube with macaroni. Here, the richly flavoured beef is spooned over wide ribbons of egg pasta, and accompanied by one of the region's most famous side dishes, garlicky baked tomatoes. Begin the meal with a savoury onion tart best served at room temperature, conclude with a French patisserie favourite that requires no work at all on your part – chocolate éclairs – and you have a meal with staying power.

Menu for 6

Pissaladière

Memories of *Lyon Beef Daube*

Herbed Pappardelle

Baked Tomatoes with Garlic and Parsley

PC *Frozen Miniature Chocolate Éclairs*

The wine – medium mellow red southern France or Spain

Allow 4 1/2 hours. Make daube. Prepare onions for pissaladière (do not assemble). Assemble tomatoes. Bake pissaladière. Bake tomatoes. Transfer éclairs to refrigerator. Reheat daube. Serve room-temperature pissaladière. Cook pasta.

Memories of Lyon Beef Daube

Beef braised in a rich wine sauce takes its name from the covered casserole, or daubière, in which it is traditionally cooked.

3 lb (1.5 kg)	stewing beef, cut in chunks
2	shallots, finely chopped
2	carrots, finely chopped
1 cup (250 mL)	red wine
1 1/2 cups (375 mL)	*PC Memories of* Lyon 4-Peppercorn Sauce
1 1/2 cups (375 mL)	water
2 tsp (10 mL)	*PC* Fresh Concentrated Beef Stock
2 tbsp (25 mL)	chopped fresh thyme

1. Preheat oven to 325°F (160°C).

2. In Dutch oven, combine beef, shallots, carrots, red wine, sauce, water, beef stock concentrate and thyme. Bring mixture to a boil on the stove, stirring. Cover pan and transfer to oven. Bake for 2 1/2 hours or until the meat is fork-tender.

3. Strain the stew, reserving liquid. Return liquid to Dutch oven. Skim fat from surface. Bring liquid to a boil, reduce heat to simmer and cook for 10 minutes, occasionally skimming off any fat and froth that floats to the surface, or until liquid is reduced by half. Return meat and vegetables to liquid, reheat gently over medium heat, stirring constantly. Serve over Herbed Pappardelle.

Makes 8 servings.

Per serving: calories 325; protein 38 g; fat 16 g; carbohydrate 7.2 g; sodium 523 mg

Daube can be prepared day ahead. Refrigerate. Reheat gently on stove, stirring constantly.

Baked Tomatoes with Garlic and Parsley

A flavourful addition to any meal.

2 tbsp (25 mL)	finely chopped fresh parsley
1 tbsp (15 mL)	*PC* Chopped Garlic in Oil
3	vine-ripened tomatoes, cut in half crosswise and cores removed
2 tbsp (25 mL)	*PC* Italian-Style Breadcrumbs with Parmesan and Romano Cheeses
1 tbsp (15 mL)	*PC Splendido* Extra Virgin Olive Oil
	Salt and freshly ground black pepper

1. Preheat oven to 325°F (160°C). Spray 8-inch (2 L) square baking dish with cooking spray.

2. Mix together parsley and garlic.

3. Arrange tomato halves cut side up in prepared dish. Top with parsley-garlic mixture, then with breadcrumbs. Drizzle with olive oil.

4. Bake for 1 hour or until tomatoes are slightly shrivelled and any liquid at the bottom of the baking dish is absorbed. Season with salt and pepper to taste.

Makes 6 servings.

Per serving: calories 50; protein 0.9 g; fat 2.9 g; carbohydrate 5.0 g; sodium 90 mg

Herbed Pappardelle

A simple way to dress up the delightfully wide, ribbon-like pasta called pappardelle.

1 pkg (250 g)	*PC Splendido* Pappardelle Nests
2 tbsp (25 mL)	unsalted butter
2 tbsp (25 mL)	finely chopped fresh parsley

1. In large pot of boiling, salted water, cook pappardelle for 4 minutes or until tender but firm, stirring occasionally to separate strands.

2. Drain; toss with butter and parsley. Serve immediately.

Makes 6 servings.

Per serving: calories 168; protein 5.8 g; fat 3.6 g; carbohydrate 28 g; sodium 57 mg

Pissaladière

A Canadian twist on the beloved onion tart of Southern France.

2 tbsp (25 mL)	butter
2	large red onions, thinly sliced
3 tbsp (45 mL)	*PC* 100% Pure Maple Syrup
3 tbsp (45 mL)	*PC* 8-Year-Old Balsamic Vinegar
	Salt and freshly ground black pepper
1 (425 g)	*PC Splendido* Herbes de Provence Flatbread
1 pkg (140 g)	*PC* Herbed Soft Unripened Goat's Milk Cheese
12	black olives, pitted

1. Position rack in centre of oven and preheat to 425°F (220°C).

2. In saucepan, melt butter over medium heat; cook onions for 5 minutes, stirring occasionally, or until softened. Stir in maple syrup and vinegar. Cook for 25 minutes, stirring occasionally, or until onions are tender and golden brown. Season with salt and pepper to taste.

3. Spread onion mixture evenly over flatbread. Place goat cheese in 12 small spoonfuls over surface and top each spoonful with a pitted olive.

4. Bake directly on oven rack for 10 to 12 minutes or until edges are crispy and cheese is softened. Sprinkle with additional pepper. Serve at room temperature.

Makes 6 servings.

Per serving: calories 360; protein 9.0 g; fat 12 g; carbohydrate 54 g; sodium 818 mg

PC Frozen Miniature Chocolate Éclairs

You won't strain your wrist lifting these delightfully light-textured, bite-sized pastries made with classic choux pastry and filled with real whipped cream. A ribbon of dark, chocolatey frosting tops them off.

A Time For Java...

Actually, a cup of Java, as in the diner version hailing from the days of the silver screen, isn't anything you'd want to drink. In the three or four months it used to take green coffee to reach North America from Java and Malabar, the beans had turned brown from bunking in the sweltering, humid hulls of ships. The result: all body, all strength and very little flavour!

Yet coffee is ultimately all about flavour. We clamour for a cup. We can even tolerate the occasional bad cup.

And it takes a lot to curb that desire, despite the many serious attempts made through the centuries for religious or political reasons. Mahomet Kolpii of 16th-century Egypt hired thugs and vandals to deter patrons, and when that didn't work, he bundled proprietors and their customers into leather sacks and cast them into the sea. This, too, failed. Like the crema, or froth, on a well-made espresso, coffee continually rises above the efforts to ban it from the table.

A little history, in brief

They say the Arab goatherd Kaldi discovered coffee on the Arabian peninsula (now called Yemen) about the same time work began on the *Arabian Nights* (c. 800 AD), back when Baghdad was the seat of world power. However, the first tree likely sprang up in central Ethiopia, and made its way across the Red Sea to Kaldi's grazing grounds during a single generation of Ethiopian rule. At first the brew was made by steeping dried green beans in the same manner as tea. Roasting came later. Today, there is a bean, a roast, a grind and a drip cone, pot or plunger to suit every culture.

Portrait of a good bean

No matter what your preference, experts agree that the smoothest-tasting coffee begins with Arabica beans from the original coffee tree, *Coffea arabica*. It's said that most of the Arabica trees presently growing in Central and South America sprang from a single tree planted in 1715 by Louis XIV of France – in a greenhouse constructed specially for it.

Robustas come from the much hardier *Coffea robusta* tree, which needs far less nurturing, grows more easily at lower altitudes, and is almost immune to the elements. (Just as wine and other fruits of the earth can have their off years, so can coffee, and it's all attributable to weather.) But compared to Arabica beans, robustas taste harsh. Does your coffee turn grey when you add cream? Either it has sat on the coffee-pot burner too long or the blend was full of robustas. The best place for robustas is in Italian espresso, where a small percentage can help create a good crema, or brown foam.

The measure of a good coffee

If only your coffee could talk! Well, it can. You'd be surprised at what you can learn just by opening up a tin and reading the grinds. First, there's the aroma: A sour, earthy or nondescript toasty smell pretty much indicates what you'll end up with in the cup. One sniff should say 'coffee.' Then there's the appearance. Jerry Rogers, our *President's Choice* green-coffee buyer whose buying expeditions once took him to 93 coffee-producing countries in a single year, can read coffee like a book. "Open a quality coffee and you'll see that the colour is dark brown," he says. "You have to roast fine-quality beans darker to get the best character out of them. Some buyers underroast on purpose because they start with poorer quality beans, and those would end up tasting harsh. The other thing to look for is consistency in the grind; there shouldn't be any large chunks visible."

Pouring some lower-grade ground coffee out onto a sheet of white paper, Jerry points to the putty-coloured chunks. "What really stands out are these very light pieces of coffee. The cheaper the blend, the more you'll see – they look like sawdust. These light pieces are from coffees that were not mature when harvested. The beans weren't red, which means they weren't ripe. They can be *almost* red and they will roast up *almost* to a normal colour. But they've got a harsh character, not coffee-like at all. It's usually from coffee that was stripped from the trees, instead of being picked one berry at a time when red. So you get ripe, unripe and everything in between. Unripe beans can never roast up to a dark brown. They stay quite lightish in colour, like a peanut. A premium roaster won't accept them in the blend even though they're cheaper. Black beans are overripe, and can impart a sour, bitter, fermented taste to the blend. For higher quality coffee, roasters will require that all defective beans, light or dark, be removed by electronic sorting machines or, in some instances, by hand."

Coffee caretaking

Whether green or roasted, coffee absorbs odours like a sponge, and ground coffee even more so. So always keep it in an airtight container in a cool, dark place. You can store an opened tin of ground coffee in the refrigerator for two to three weeks, the same for whole beans. But if you have a month's worth of beans, store them in the freezer. They can be ground from frozen. Avoid blender-like coffee grinders for it's impossible to control the consistency of grind in these units. Coffee should be ground in one pass, not be partly pulverized by whirling blades. A powdery grind is a problem since the finer the grind, the faster the rate of extraction.

Show a healthy respect for bean freshness, but don't let an obsession for it rob you of coffee enjoyment. Every step it

takes to get coffee from the tree to your table unavoidably contributes to its loss of flavour. So unless you can somehow roast, grind, brew and drink it in one go, you're looking for the Holy Grail.

Brewing style

The bean meets up with personal style at the time of brewing.

A programmable automatic-drip coffee maker, ideally with a thermal carafe to keep it hot, will let you wake up to the aroma of fresh brewed coffee every morning. Espresso drinkers prefer the jolt from a shot of strong, hot coffee taken standing up, with sugar or a twist of lemon rind. Good crema is a sign of well-made espresso. When you sprinkle sugar over the foam, it should sit on top for about three seconds. You can use medium to dark roasts – use it in a drip coffee maker too. Drip coffee makers are fast, but your heart will be with the plunger pot, or French press, if you want ease of brewing as well as a veil of tan foam on the surface to show that this is no ordinary cup. There are flavour elements in coffee that give it body and texture, and a plunger pot allows more of these substances to remain in the brew. To keep the coffee warm while it steeps, wrap a clean, folded-up tea towel around the pot.

The following constants apply, whichever brewing method you use:

- Keep your coffee maker clean.
- Use quality coffee and fresh-drawn water (filtered, if possible).
- Use the correct grind: regular for plunger pots and percolators, fine grind for automatic drip coffee makers, and extra-fine grind for espresso or manual drip coffee makers.
- For flavour and body, use about 2 level tablespoons (25 mL) of ground coffee for every 3/4 cup (175 mL) of water. If somebody wants a weaker-tasting cup, dilute the brewed coffee with boiling water. For a stronger cup, use 3 level tablespoons (45 mL) ground coffee to the same amount of water.
- To ensure even flavour distribution in every cup, stir the pot before pouring.

Almost like wine

Like wine, coffee tastes of the soil in which it is grown. But with coffee, you can blend as many varieties as your heart desires from as many different parts of the world as you wish. And what a range there is, as Jerry Rogers discovered during a stopover in Germany more than 30 years ago. "In Europe, and particularly Germany – Scandinavia is similar – you have many coffee shops with fine coffees from all over the world, roasted, in whole bean form, sold in bins. They had a broader base of coffees than even our specialty shops today. There was coffee from Indonesia, East Africa, the islands of Java, Sumatra, Celebes, and then all of Central America and some South America. One shop in Hamburg had more than 1,500 regular customers with their own blends, and some might have five or six countries of origin in a single recipe." With about 60 coffee-producing countries in the world, each with three to 12 different qualities of beans, there are thousands of combinations to play with.

Coffee for a crowd

Thermal pump pots are best for keeping coffee hot for a crowd since the flavour stays fresh for up to two hours, says Jerry Rogers. To make and hold coffee in an aluminum urn, prepare it no more than 20 to 30 minutes ahead. The amount of ground coffee needed might look like a lot, but it's not. For a mild-tasting cup from a 30-cup urn (3/4 cup/175 mL portions), expect to use 2 1/2 cups (625 mL) of *PC Club Pack* regular grind gourmet coffee.

'I am glad I wasn't born before tea'

British writer Sydney Smith (1771-1845)

Tea is completely fascinating. It's the most consumed beverage in the world next to water, but you can't gulp it down while you're on the phone and do it any justice. Simply breathing in its fragrance can be like taking a journey to a faraway place. A green tea carries the leafy scent of the plant itself; a Russian tea can be as smokey as tobacco. There's a maltiness to Assam, while Darjeeling carries a sweet muscat grape scent. Aside from its beguiling aromas, tea helps slow down time. The mere act of drinking tea requires time to appreciate its pleasing nuances of flavour.

According to Chinese legend, Emperor Shen Nung, himself possibly a legend, discovered "tea" in 2737 BC, when a willow leaf dropped into his cup of hot water as he sat relaxing in his garden. Brick tea was available in Japan by 593, and a Korean envoy took seeds back home with him after a posting in China in the early 900s. Zen Buddhist monks from China introduced tea to Japan when they took it along for temple ceremonies. Tea reached Holland in 1610 and arrived in England in 1644, where it was served up in coffee houses. From there, the world was quickly conquered.

In China today, people greet each other on the street with "Have you had tea yet?" even before they say hello. That country's tea ceremony is like a comfortable tea tasting compared to Japan's highly structured "The Way of Tea," for which one must go to school to learn the rules. The Koreans call tea The Dew of Wisdom (panyaro), and are as excited about the first growth of the year as the French are by fresh young Beaujolais.

A tale of two teas

Whether it's green or black, all tea comes from the leaves of the same evergreen bush, *Camellia sinensis*. Green tea leaves are steamed and dried within 24 hours to prevent the juices from oxidizing, or fermenting, while oxidation is used to develop flavour in black teas.

Steeping and boiling methods differ for green and black teas. To protect colour and nutritional values, and prevent bitterness, green tea should be made using water barely at the boil and be allowed to steep only for 3 minutes, tops. Black teas need a full rolling boil to release their flavour.

Herbal teas aren't really teas at all but infusions of plant leaves, stems, bark and berries. In Europe, they're called tisanes, and often consumed for therapeutic reasons, aside from their uplifting flavours.

The afternoon refreshment

The term "tea" to describe Britain's afternoon institution was not used until the mid-1600s. Its first mention came into use when the Seventh Duchess of Bedford asked her butler for a cup of tea and something to eat to tide her over to a late-evening dinner. It proved so agreeable that she began inviting friends over to join her. A tea is still a wonderful way to entertain special friends. But first, a few pointers:

- Invest in a good tea pot that can hold the heat. Some come with their own infusing chambers for loose tea.
- Warm the pot with boiling water.
- Use a good quality tea.
- Give black tea sufficient time to steep, at least 3 to 5 minutes. If using bagged tea, don't be too quick to remove it from the pot. The colour is extracted before any of its flavour components.
- Remove tea bags before pouring.

The Best Tea For The Occasion

Teas vary in their flavour characteristics. As a result, many people are discovering that tea can complement foods in the way that wines do. To discover this phenomenon yourself, try these food pairings:

PC Green Tea (refreshing): all foods, especially noodles, vegetarian burgers, hummus sandwiches, Asian food, sushi, tropical fruits.

PC Orange Pekoe (black-tea blend): pastries, tomato sandwiches, sausages, cheesecake, lemon tart.

PC Earl Grey (scented with bergamot): pâtés, biscuits, ham-and-mustard sandwiches, crème brulée.

PC Assam (full-bodied and brisk): bacon and eggs, scones, blue cheese, old Cheddar cheese, beef, smoked cheeses, chocolate cake.

PC Darjeeling (light tasting, best plain): smoked salmon, cucumber or chicken salad sandwiches, mild Cheddar cheese, cream cheese, apple pie.

An Italian Holiday Table

Holiday cheer at this festive table comes in three colours – green, white and red, the colours of the Italian flag – which constitute a warm introduction to the celebrations. They reflect the most refined sentiments of the season, since green stands for hope, white for faith, and red for charity.

Natale (Christmas) is a two-day feast in Italy, and the celebrating runs until the Feast of Epiphany on January 6, when everybody finally gets to open their gifts.

Fish or seafood makes its customary appearance in this menu since on *Le Vigilia* (the eve) most families respect the church rule to eat lean (*mangiare di magro*). But that doesn't mean fasting foods can't be luxurious. Oven risotto is luxurious, and doubly so with sweet shrimp in it. 'Pasta' appears as sweet pepper 'cannelloni' with a surprise filling, while the sauté of broccoli with garlic is traditional for the occasion. The timbales are strictly our fancy.

Oranges make a refreshing dessert and would be one of the foods traditionally available in an Italian marketplace during this season. Crunchy biscotti are eaten year round in Italy but are also one of its most famous holiday foods. As for cannoli, we learned that some of the best are to be had in Sicily because Sicilians wait until the last moment to fill the crisp pastry shells with ricotta and chopped chocolate.

Oh, one other thing. While the sound of sleigh bells is music to our ears, the holiday background theme in Italy is supplied by minstrel sheep herders who come down from the mountains to play their bagpipes and flutes in the streets of the cities. *Buon Natale!*

Menu for 8

Oven Risotto with Peas and Shrimp

Meatballs with Red Wine and Onions

Sweet Pepper 'Cannelloni'

Broccoli Spears all'aglio

Rösti Potato Timbales

Spiced Orange and Cranberry Salad

PC Splendido *Frozen Mini Cannoli*

PC *Almond Biscotti*

The wine – a medium Italian red
Chianti or barbera

Thaw cannoli in refrigerator overnight. Allow 2 1/2 hours for meal. Make dressing and arrange orange salad; chill. Make timbales and meatballs. Assemble cannelloni and risotto; bake. Parboil broccoli. Reheat timbales. Sauté broccoli. Fill cannoli.

Oven Risotto with Peas and Shrimp

Consider vegetables as potential garnishes. In the photo, pencil-thin asparagus form a wreath around a creamy, oven-cooked risotto.

2 tbsp (25 mL)	*PC* Fresh Concentrated Chicken Stock
5 cups (1.25 L)	boiling water
2 tbsp (25 mL)	*PC Splendido* Extra Virgin Olive Oil
2 cups (500 mL)	chopped onions
2 tsp (10 mL)	*PC* Chopped Garlic in Oil
1 pkg (454 g)	*PC* Italian Arborio Super Fino Rice
1 cup (250 mL)	dry white wine
1/2 tsp (2 mL) each	salt and freshly ground black pepper
2 cups (500 mL)	*PC* Frozen Petits Pois
1 pkg (300 g)	*PC* Frozen Tomato & Herb Skillet Shrimp
1/2 cup (125 mL)	finely chopped fresh parsley
2 tbsp (25 mL)	unsalted butter

1. Preheat oven to 350°F (180°C).
2. Dissolve chicken stock concentrate in boiling water.
3. In ovenproof saucepan, heat oil over medium heat. Cook onions and garlic for 3 to 5 minutes or until onions are transparent. Add rice. Cook, stirring, for 2 to 3 minutes or until rice is well-coated with oil. Add wine. Cook for 2 minutes, stirring, or until wine is absorbed. Add chicken stock. Bring to a boil; continue to boil, stirring constantly, for 3 minutes. Stir in salt and pepper. Cover pan tightly; transfer to oven. Bake for 10 minutes.
4. Remove pan from oven. Stir in peas and shrimp. Cover and bake 20 to 25 minutes longer, or until rice is creamy but still firm to the bite, and shrimp are cooked through.
5. Vigorously stir in parsley and butter, and serve immediately.

Makes 8 servings.

Per serving: calories 381; protein 9.1 g; fat 12 g; carbohydrate 59 g; sodium 756 mg

Meatballs with Red Wine and Onions

Most of the alcohol in the wine evaporates during cooking, leaving behind thin but richly flavoured pan juices.

1 tsp (5 mL)	*PC* Fresh Concentrated Beef Stock
1 cup (250 mL)	boiling water
1 tbsp (15 mL)	unsalted butter
2 cups (500 mL)	chopped onions
1 box (907 g)	*PC* Frozen Italian-Style Meatballs
1 cup (250 mL)	red wine
1/4 tsp (1 mL) each	salt and freshly ground black pepper

1. Dissolve beef stock concentrate in boiling water.
2. In large saucepan, melt butter over medium heat; cook onions for 5 minutes or until tender. Stir in frozen meatballs, wine, salt, pepper and beef stock. Bring to a boil. Reduce heat to low. Cover and cook for 45 minutes, stirring occasionally.
3. Transfer to serving dish.

Makes 8 servings.

Per serving: calories 343; protein 19 g; fat 23 g; carbohydrate 15 g; sodium 784 mg

Broccoli Spears all'aglio

Italian cooks sauté many vegetables in olive oil and garlic (aglio), especially greens.

1 pkg (1 kg)	*PC* Frozen Premium Quality Broccoli Spears
2 tbsp (25 mL)	*PC Splendido* Extra Virgin Olive Oil
2 tbsp (25 mL)	*PC* Chopped Garlic in Oil
	Salt and freshly ground black pepper

1. In large pot of boiling, salted water, cook broccoli for 3 to 5 minutes or until tender-crisp; drain. Refresh under cold running water; drain.
2. In large frying pan, heat oil over medium-high heat. Cook garlic, stirring, for 30 seconds. Do not brown. Add broccoli; cook for 5 minutes, stirring gently, or until heated through and coated with oil and garlic. Season with salt and pepper to taste.

Makes 8 servings.

Per serving: calories 83; protein 3.7 g; fat 4.3 g; carbohydrate 7.3 g; sodium 76 mg

Rösti Potato Timbales

In Switzerland, rösti means "crisp and golden." To us it means shredded potatoes ready to bake up into individual moulds.

4	eggs
1/2 cup (125 mL)	18% table cream
1 cup (250 mL)	shredded *PC Splendido* Partly Skimmed Stretched Mozzarella Cheese
1 pkg (567 g)	*PC* Swiss-Style Rösti
1/4 tsp (1 mL)	freshly ground black pepper

1. Preheat oven to 350°F (180°C). Lightly oil 12-cup muffin tin; dust with flour.
2. In bowl, whisk eggs for 1 minute. Whisk in cream. Stir in cheese, rösti and pepper. Divide mixture evenly among prepared muffin cups.
3. Bake for 25 to 30 minutes or until set and golden.
4. To lift out, gently run knife around edges of timbales.

Makes 12 servings.

Per timbale: calories 113; protein 6.2 g; fat 5 g; carbohydrate 11 g; sodium 255 mg

Can be made day ahead. Refrigerate. Reheat in microwave oven on Medium High for 1 1/2 to 2 1/2 minutes.

Sweet Pepper 'Cannelloni'

Bright and sunny looking, with a surprise tucked inside.

4	sweet peppers (2 red, 2 yellow)
1	small portobello mushroom
1 1/2 cups (375 mL)	*PC Splendido* Original *Italian Magic* Sauce
1 pkg (140 g)	*PC* Soft Unripened Goat's Milk Cheese, divided into 8 portions
2 tsp (10 mL)	*PC Splendido* Grated 100% Italian Parmesan Cheese

1. Preheat oven to 350°F (180°C).
2. Cut peppers in half lengthwise. Remove seed cores. Add peppers to large pot of boiling, salted water. Cook for 10 minutes. Drain. Let cool.
3. Remove mushroom stem. Wipe cap clean. Cut into 1/4-inch (5 mm) wide strips the length of peppers.
4. Pour 1 cup (250 mL) of the *Italian Magic* into 8-inch (2 L) square baking dish.
5. Place mushroom strip and one portion of goat cheese lengthwise inside each pepper. Fold peppers in half to encase filling. Place in baking dish, alternating red and yellow peppers. Pour remaining *Italian Magic* in broad ribbon across peppers. Sprinkle *Italian Magic* with Parmesan.
6. Bake for 20 to 25 minutes.

Makes 8 servings.

Per serving: calories 87; protein 3.8 g; fat 4.1 g; carbohydrate 8.7 g; sodium 350 mg

Can be assembled day ahead to point of baking. Refrigerate.

Spiced Orange and Cranberry Salad

Sliced oranges are the basis of a refreshing dessert salad.

4	oranges
1/4 cup (50 mL)	*PC* Cranberry 100% Juice
2 tbsp (25 mL)	*PC* Premium Alfalfa Honey
1/4 tsp (1 mL)	ground ginger
1/2 cup (125 mL)	*PC* Raisin-Cranberry Portage Mix, roughly chopped

1. Peel oranges; gently break into halves. Cut each half crosswise into thin slices. Arrange attractively on serving platter.
2. In small bowl, whisk cranberry juice, honey and ginger.
3. Just before serving, sprinkle oranges with Portage Mix and pour cranberry juice mixture over top.

Makes 8 servings.

Per serving: calories 117; protein 2.5 g; fat 3.4 g; carbohydrate 19 g; sodium 25 mg

Can be prepared night before. Refrigerate oranges and dressing separately.

PC _Splendido_ _Frozen Mini Cannoli_

Traditional cannoli shells, like these, are made with white wine in the batter, and filled just before serving with a sweetened ricotta cheese-and-chocolate chip mixture. For a real Italian touch, dust with icing sugar before serving.

PC _Almond Biscotti_

Our Italian import is studded with almonds and baked until crisp. Perfect for serving alongside coffee or dessert wines such as vin santo.

New Year's Cocktail Soirée

You've come to the end of the year. Now it's time for auld lang syne, an opportunity to spend a few hours with people you've been too busy to see most of the year. And you can't do that if you're locked away in the kitchen cooking. A cocktail soirée is an opportunity to get together, however briefly, and hail thee all well. This menu relies on *President's Choice* frozen finger foods – ready-to-heat hors d'oeuvre and tiny pastries that your friends can enjoy at a before- or after-dinner get-together. A mood of informality prevails, since most of the work is in shopping and setting up. What a nice change from waving hello and goodbye from across the kitchen island!

Menu for 8 to 10

THE SAVOURIES

Accompanied by full-flavoured Champagne brut or Spiced Sparkling Cranberry-Apple Punch (non-alcoholic).

PC Frozen Escargots en Brioche – French-style yeast breads filled with escargots in a garlic butter sauce. *225 g, 12 pieces*

PC Splendido Frozen Crostini Selection topped with three cheeses – roasted 4-vegetable, roasted 3-mushroom, and tomato & basil. *260 g, 15 pieces*

PC Frozen Shrimp Spring Rolls with *PC Memories of* Canton Hot Plum Sauce. *510 g, 24 pieces*

PC Frozen Silver Platter Quiche Collection – cheese & ham, broccoli & cheddar, and Italian-style quiches *255 g, 12 pieces*

PC Frozen 40-Piece Cheese Hors d'Oeuvre Collection – cheese & onion puffs, mushroom & cheese triangles, cheese, tomato and pesto crescents and cheese & spinach puffs. *800 g*

PC Frozen Brie & Cranberry Filo Parcels *280 g, 16 pieces*

PC Smoked Salmon & Spinach Mousse *200 g*

PC Biscuits for Cheese *500 g*

PC Frozen Double Black Tiger Shrimp Ring and *PC* Tangy Seafood Sauce *800 g*

Vegetable tray with *PC Too Good To Be True* Fat Free Tzatziki Yogurt Dip and Spread. *250 g tub*

THE SWEETS

Accompanied by Canadian icewine or late harvest wine, or Darjeeling Eggfree Eggnog (non-alcoholic).

PC Frozen Mini Cream Cheese & 3-Berry Filo Bundles – bite-sized bundles with raspberries, blueberries and strawberries inside. *195 g, 12 pieces*

PC Celebration European Biscuit Assortment *1 kg, 15 varieties*

PC The Decadent Frozen Mini Chocolate Collection – Mocha Mousse Swirl, Grand Marnier Chocolate Truffles, Chocolate Hazelnut Logs, Tiramisu. *175 g, 16 pieces*

PC Frozen Mini Apple Strudel Filo Rolls – bite-sized rolls with Northern Spy apples, almonds, Sultana raisins and cinnamon. *360 g, 12 pieces*

PC Almond Crunch Cookies and *PC* Dutch Butter Cookies *200 g each*

Spiced Sparkling Cranberry-Apple Punch

Float a few orange slices on top for even more colour.

1/2 cup (125 mL)	fresh or frozen cranberries
	Water
3 cups (750 mL)	*PC* Fresh-Pressed Sweet Apple Cider
4	cinnamon sticks
6 cups (1.5 L)	*PC* Sparkling Cranberry Juice, chilled

1. Place one cranberry in each compartment of an ice cube tray. Fill with water. Freeze until solid.

2. Pour apple cider into pitcher. Add cinnamon sticks and remaining cranberries. Chill, covered, for at least 2 hours.

3. Just before serving, empty contents of pitcher into punch bowl (do not strain). Add cranberry ice cubes. Pour in sparkling cranberry juice.

Makes 12 servings.

Per serving: calories 92; protein 0.1 g; fat 0 g; carbohydrate 23 g; sodium 1.2 mg

Cider mixture can be prepared day ahead. Add sparkling cranberry juice and cranberry ice cubes at time of serving.

Get Ready To Ring In The New

These entertaining tips, most of which are drawn from *PC* Chef Michelle Irwin's own experience, are worth practising all year round.

- Make lots of lists. Decide on the guests. Draw up a shopping list and preparation timetable – for a week in advance if necessary. This will help you pace yourself.

- Decide if you have all the serving supplies you require. Almost anything can be rented – glasses, coffee cups, plates, cutlery, table linens, chairs or a small folding table for coffee and beverages. (Check every piece before it goes back to the rental place to make sure your favourite platters aren't in there.)

- Provide guests with a good mix of foods, textures and temperatures: hot, cold, seafood, vegetarian, chicken, beef, rich, light, etc. It helps to include vegetables as an alternative to rich-tasting dishes. If you intend to do any cooking, write down the source and page number when jotting down recipe ideas, so you can retrieve them quickly.

- Plan as many low-maintenance food items as possible, such as cheese trays (see page 90), vegetable trays and dips, a shrimp ring and sauce, etc. There's no heating involved, and they are all easy to replenish. The foods can be arranged and garnished ahead of time, and kept refrigerated until you need them.

- Plan on each guest eating 4 to 6 hors d'oeuvre per hour during mealtimes. Don't include shrimp in this count. The shrimp is always the first item to disappear, no matter how much other food is served! Set a small bowl beside the shrimp ring so people know where to put the tails.

- For the sweets table, plan on fewer pieces per person than hors d'oeuvre. Do include fresh fruit as most people enjoy something lighter to finish off.

- Provide a delicious non-alcoholic beverage for your guests. For our New Year's Cocktail Soirée, we offer two suggestions, one a sparkling cranberry-apple punch (page 132) served with hors d'oeuvre and the other an exotic eggnog made with Darjeeling tea (page 136) for the sweets table.

- Have supplies of water or sparkling mineral water on hand.

- Place cocktail napkins in fanned-out stacks near the food and around the room so they're always within reach and easy to pick up.

- Keep music subdued so it doesn't interfere with conversation. And be sure to pick a style of music that's appropriate to the occasion! Marching bands or certain forms of jazz can leave nerves feeling jangled.

- Hors d'oeuvre can be passed or placed on a buffet. Guests will always find trays of food on tables but it's a nice touch to pass warm hors d'oeuvre so that people can carry on their conversations.

- Keep an eye on the beverage situation. Replenish white wine bottles in ice buckets and ice for drinks. Have red wine in glasses on trays so guests can help themselves. Or walk through, refilling glasses. Replenish water.

- Make coffee to serve with dessert, and be prepared to make tea for those who prefer it. Give them the option. An extra coffee thermos comes in handy for holding decaffeinated or flavoured coffee.

- Do a walk-through every 30 minutes or so to check on guests, and clear up as you go along. Pick up stray cocktail napkins, abandoned glasses, empty plates, and full ashtrays, if smoking is allowed.

- Do as much as you can in advance. The reason for getting together with friends is to enjoy their company!

Setting The Mood

There are many ways to decorate a table or platter.

- Try to incorporate different levels on your buffet. If you're short on cake stands, build height beneath the tablecloth. Use books or other objects large enough to support your platters, then drape a tablecloth over all.

- Use candles of different sizes, heights and widths to create ambiance.

- Make frosted fruit to garnish serving plates and table. Use edible flower petals if you can find them (violets, rose petals, etc.). To frost a few clusters of red currants or tiny red grapes, beat one egg white lightly with a fork. Gently brush beaten egg white all over the fruit and stems; transfer the coated fruit to a plateful of fruit sugar (an extra-fine granulated sugar), and spoon over more sugar to coat the fruit evenly. Gently shake off the excess sugar and set sugared fruit on parchment or waxed paper until dry. Refrigerate until needed. Do not cover or the sugar will dissolve.

- Let your imagination loose. Use fresh flowers or even vegetables to create unusual table decorations.

- Take advantage of seasonal fruits, too, for table decorations. Scatter kumquats randomly for effect. Or decorate the table with pomegranates or pears, such as Forelles or small red Seckel pears. Fill bowls with clementines, which are not only sweet and delicious, but very easy to eat at a buffet. Oranges or clementines studded with whole cloves look and smell deliciously seasonal.

- Use ribbon! Tying a wide ribbon around a tray of assorted nuts and candies – or even a shrimp ring platter – will make them presentable for a festive table.

- Cinnamon sticks can be bundled up with ribbon to add height to a table setting. Broken in pieces, cinnamon sticks are a garnish for eggnog (add a sprinkle of ground cinnamon to complete the effect). Or use them as stir-sticks for the spiced punch.

- Try to make foods both functional and attractive. For example, put cucumber sticks into lemon halves for a vegetable tray (see photo on page 139).

A Sweet Finish

You can entertain guests mid-afternoon or after the dinner hour with coffee or other beverages, and an assortment of miniature sweets. Or let sweets follow savouries. If serving hors d'oeuvre, reset the buffet for dessert, or use a table in another room for a change of scenery.

30 minutes ahead

Position rack in middle of oven. Preheat oven to 400°F (200°C). Start brewing coffee, according to the size of your coffee pot, and particularly if you are using an urn. Set out coffee cups and teaspoons.

15 minutes ahead

Transfer *PC* frozen chocolates to serving plate to thaw. Put out the cream and sugar. Put out a bowl of fresh fruit or a tray of fresh-cut fruit. Be prepared to make tea for guests who want it.

Line baking sheet for frozen sweet pastries, or use a non-stick baking sheet. Bake cream cheese-berry bundles for 8 to 10 minutes. Bake apple-strudel filos for about 12 minutes. Remove the pastries from oven and place briefly on paper towel before transferring to serving dish.

Darjeeling Eggfree Eggnog

A holiday classic revisited – a delicious non-alcoholic version.

10 tea bags	*PC* Darjeeling Tea
4 cups (1 L)	boiling water
2 cans (600 mL)	*PC* Sweetened Condensed Milk
4 cups (1 L)	milk
2 cups (500 mL)	18% table cream
2 tsp (10 mL)	vanilla
1/2 tsp (2 mL)	freshly grated nutmeg

1. Steep tea bags in boiling water for 10 minutes.
2. Strain tea into large pitcher; stir in condensed milk, milk, cream, vanilla and nutmeg. Refrigerate for 3 hours or until well chilled.

Makes 10 servings.

Per serving: calories 328; protein 8.5 g; fat 14 g; carbohydrate 42 g; sodium 140 mg

Countdown To A New Year

Weeks ahead

Draw up your guest list and send out invitations. Socializing is intense at year-end, and people like to make plans early. To ensure your order for rented party supplies can be filled, place it as soon as possible. Reconfirm at least two weeks ahead. If serving mixed drinks, you may wish to hire a bartender.

Up to a week ahead

Multiply the number of guests by the number of hors d'oeuvre you will need (4 to 6 pieces per hour, per guest, during the "hungry" hour). Decide if you want to include a cheese tray with the hot hors d'oeuvre. Shop for frozen or pantry products to make sure you get the best selection. Stock up on wine, as well as spring water and mineral water. Stop by a bulk spice shop to pick up cinnamon sticks, peppercorns and cloves for table decorations.

Necessary equipment

2 baking sheets, and aluminum foil or cooking parchment to line them with. Lining pans reduces the transfer of flavours when you are heating up a variety of foods in assembly-line fashion. Plus, there's less cleanup.

Day before

Make sure platters, plates and glasses are sparkling clean. Inspect silverware to see if it needs polishing. You don't want any last-minute surprises! Pick up any rental supplies.

Figure out where ice buckets for white wine will go, and set glasses in the same area. Red wine can be poured during the party and placed on trays for guests to help themselves, or the tray can be passed around.

Lay the buffet tables while there's time to think about where everything should go. (Use small sticky notes as reminders.) Cover serving plates and glasses loosely with napkins or paper towels to keep

dust off. Arrange centrepieces and candlesticks. Fold the cocktail napkins or arrange in fanned-out stacks on the buffet table and around room.

If you're not buying ice, start making ice cubes and store in bags in freezer.

Night before

Prepare carrots for vegetable trays (peel but leave on some stem for a garden-fresh look). Wash cherry tomatoes and make flowerets from cauliflower and broccoli. If desired, parboil broccoli to bring the colour up – 1 to 2 minutes in a large pot of boiling, salted water or until it turns vivid green – then immediately plunge into bowl of ice water. Refrigerate.

Wash and dry herbs for garnishes; wrap in paper towel and put in vegetable bin of refrigerator. Make cranberry ice cubes and cider base for punch (do not add sparkling juice yet). Make the eggnog; refrigerate, covered. Thaw shrimp ring in its packaging.

Bundle up cinnamon sticks and tie with a ribbon. Decorate oranges or clementines by inserting cloves in attractive patterns.

Now, sit down and relax.

Morning of the party

Don't forget the ice if you're not making your own! Buy at least two 5.95-lb (2.7 kg) bags to fill ice buckets, and extra to fill up a sink to keep soft drinks, wine and beer cold. (If weather permits, you can store the ice outside.)

Find a pretty jar or container and fill it with peppercorns; wrap the top with a pretty ribbon. Insert wooden skewers and, using scissors, cut skewers to fit the height of jar. Spear small fresh artichokes and arrange to resemble a bouquet.

Tuck a sprig of fresh mint into ribbon holding bundle of cinnamon sticks.

This is another good spot to sit down, put your feet up, and have a tea or coffee...

Do all last-minute shopping – flowers, fresh baguettes (or other breads) for the smoked salmon-spinach mousse and cheese tray if necessary. Arrange flowers and prepare vegetable and cheese trays. Remember that some cheeses need to be put out the morning of the party or midday. Your cheese seller can advise you.

3 hours ahead

Make cucumber cups and cucumber sticks to use as plate garnishes for the savoury table. If desired, score cucumber cups with a citrus zester to make stripes or run the tines of a fork down the skin. Keep the cucumber garnishes on a plate, covered with a damp paper towel and loosely covered with plastic, and refrigerate.

Make "frosted" or sugar-coated fruit for garnishing the sweets table (see page 135).

1 hour ahead

Put out cheese tray, loosely covered, if including. Arrange cookies on plates. Garnish plates and table with sugar-coated fruit. An optional addition (not pictured) are bowls of nuts – *PC* Butter Toffee Peanuts, *PC* Party Peanuts, *PC* Deluxe Mixed Nuts and/or *PC* Roasted Whole Cashews.

30 minutes ahead

Time to start heating the frozen hors d'oeuvre. The following schedule will help your timing, but don't panic! Remember, hot foods don't all have to be ready at the same time. What's important is to establish the "flow." Don't worry about food shortages. The cold foods will keep your guests occupied.

Position top and bottom racks to divide oven into thirds. Preheat oven to 425°F (220°C).

- Place cheese collection (12-14 minutes), shrimp spring rolls (12-14 minutes), and crostini (10 to 12 minutes) on lined baking sheets. Space evenly apart. Put pastries in preheated 425°F (220°C) oven – crostini and spring rolls on lower rack, cheese pastries on top rack. Check on crostini first since they'll be done a couple of minutes before the others. Remove each from oven when ready, and transfer to serving dishes.

- Leave oven door ajar briefly and reduce heat to 400°F (200°C) while you reline baking sheets. Place cranberry-Brie filos on lined sheet, then put on top rack in oven. When golden (about 8 minutes), remove from oven and transfer to serving dish.

- Leave oven door ajar briefly and reduce heat to 375°F (190°C) while you reline baking sheet for quiches. When heated (12 to 15 minutes), transfer quiches to serving plate. For softer pastry, quiches can also be microwaved in under 4 minutes – see package directions.

- Leave oven door ajar briefly and reduce heat to 350°F (180°C). Put in escargots. When escargots are done (12 to 15 minutes), transfer to serving dish, then use the tip of a knife to offset the caps slightly to show the escargots inside (see photo on page 134).

- Leave oven on for replenishing hot hors d'oeuvre.

15 minutes ahead

Add sparkling cranberry juice to cider mixture in punch bowl. Fill ice buckets for white wine. Pour red wine into glasses and set on tray. Put out shrimp ring and a small bowl beside it so that people have a place to put the tails. Put out vegetable tray with dip. Set out bowl of plum sauce for the shrimp spring rolls. Unmould smoked salmon-spinach mousse according to package instructions, and arrange on plate with assorted crackers or slices of baguette.

You can set up a sweet or savoury table any time during the holiday season for entertaining guests.

Tips & Techniques

Kitchen smarts

Building on convenience products – the modern way to cheat in the kitchen – speeds mealtime preparation, and it has been thus ever since the first cake mix. Existing products are like a muse to the creative spirit. Ask anyone who has ever doctored up a cake mix! Consider it streamlined cooking. At its quickest, it means picking up everything from the entrée (freezer section) and side dishes and salads (hot and cold deli), to the dessert (freezer case or in-store bakery). Or you can invest time preparing a recipe that truly interests you, and fill in the rest of the meal with ready-made dishes.

This cookbook is filled with this new approach to home cooking. Here are some other suggestions:

- Take advantage of the supermarket olive bar to provide quick snacks for cocktail parties, such as these **Hot Herbed Olives:** In a frying pan, heat some extra-virgin olive oil over medium-high heat. Add a few peeled whole garlic cloves, a few large pieces of sweet red and/or yellow pepper, a sprig of fresh rosemary, cracked black pepper, and hot red pepper flakes, if desired. Sauté, stirring, for 3 to 4 minutes, then add an assortment of whole imported black and green olives. Continue sautéeing, stirring, until the olives are heated through, then transfer them to an attractive serving bowl. Don't forget to put a small bowl next to it for the pits.

- Refresh the appearance of deli pasta salads, if necessary, by mixing in fresh ingredients such as slivered sweet red peppers or sliced green onions.

- Transform plain goat cheese into **Chèvre Truffles** to liven up a cheese tray or to top a spinach salad. Using 1 tablespoon (15 mL) amounts of goat cheese, form into small balls by rolling between your palms. (A 140 g package of *PC Goat's Milk Cheese* should yield about a dozen "truffles.") Then roll them in a variety of seasonings for taste and colour – for example, paprika, cracked black pepper, toasted sesame seeds, poppy seeds, finely chopped herbs (chives, thyme or parsley), or chopped toasted nuts (walnuts, hazelnuts or macadamias). The possibilities are endless.

- Disguise store-bought desserts by dressing them up with colourful fresh fruit and fresh mint or lemon balm leaves. Just before serving, sprinkle icing sugar lightly over the entire plate. (Sieve the icing sugar first, if necessary, to remove lumps.)

- Make **Spiced Brandied Nuts** for a special occasion. Preheat oven to 375°F (190°C). Line rimmed baking sheet with aluminum foil. In a large bowl, combine 1/4 cup (50 mL) packed brown sugar, 1 tsp (5 mL) each of ground coriander and paprika, and 1/4 teaspoon (1 mL) each of allspice and cayenne. Stir in 2 tablespoons (25 mL) brandy. Add one 300 g tin *PC Deluxe Mixed Nuts.* Pour onto prepared baking sheet and bake for 10 minutes, stirring once halfway through. Remove from tray while still warm. Let cool, breaking up any clusters of nuts that may form.

- Take advantage of salad bar ingredients. It saves cleaning and preparing the vegetables, and lets you choose from a wide variety of ingredients at less cost than if you had to buy many whole fruits and vegetables.

- To make fresh fruit from a salad bar look inviting, drizzle with honey and chopped mint before serving, or scatter crushed ice over it for a Southeast Asian touch.

Storing fresh shellfish

It's worth timing a fish and seafood event to the days when your fishmonger receives fresh shipments. At any rate, buy fish and shellfish as close to the occasion as possible. Store live mussels in their mesh bag, in a bowl, in the coolest part of the refrigerator, loosely covered with a damp cloth. Do not clean mussels until you are ready to use them. Most mussels available today are cultivated, and require less cleaning than wild mussels. Use your fingers to remove the shaggy beard or trim with scissors, if necessary. Generally, cultivated mussels only need to be scrubbed and rinsed well.

To store cleaned, fresh, whole fish for a day, or up to three days if purchased very fresh (you might need to be on the pier!), place it on a plate set over a tray of ice, and cover it loosely with waxed paper. Be sure to replace the ice as it melts. Very fresh fish have clear eyes and virtually no smell. When you press them with your finger, the flesh springs back. When buying frozen fish, avoid packaging that has signs of frost, and for best flavour, thaw overnight in the refrigerator. To remove fish smells from hands, scrub them with a paste made from baking soda and water.

How to shuck an oyster

Certain varieties are easier to shuck than others. (Malpeque oysters from Prince Edward Island, for instance, are said to be one of the easier ones for beginners.) You will need an oyster knife, a small, inexpensive, wide-bladed knife. Scrub oysters well under running water. Fold a kitchen towel lengthwise in three, and place on work surface. The towel gives you a bit of a grip and protects your hands. Place the oyster rounded side down (so juices don't escape!) on one end of towel, folding other side over to cover. Insert oyster knife about 1/2 inch (1 cm) into the pointed, hinged end,

twisting the knife to pry apart the shells. Cut the muscle at the hinge, and then slide the knife underneath the oyster to loosen. Discard the top shell. Wipe the edges clean and serve immediately. Remember, a good oyster never smells bad.

Keeping foods fresh

- To store parsley whole, remove the rubber band and set the stems in a couple of inches of water in a jar or measuring cup; cover the top loosely with a plastic bag.

- Chopped parsley always comes in handy. Prepare a bunch several days ahead and refrigerate it between sheets of damp paper towel, tucked inside a resealable plastic bag.

- For leafy herbs like basil and mint, remove leaves, rinse gently, and spin-dry. Place the leaves between paper towel, slip into a resealable plastic bag, and refrigerate.

- Wash and spin-dry salad greens, then store in plastic vegetable bags (perforated resealable bags) in the vegetable bin. You can also buy airtight plastic containers for storing greens which come with a plastic rack to allow air circulation at the bottom of the container.

- Coriander is sold with the roots on. To keep it fresh in the refrigerator for several days, wrap the roots in wet paper towel and place the entire bunch in a plastic bag. Rinse coriander very well before using.

- Store potatoes, onions or shallots in a dark, dry place. If you live in an apartment, you can use a deep kitchen drawer. Don't store them under the sink, where it's damp, or in ceiling baskets, where vegetables are exposed to light. Light hastens the formation of a mild toxin on potatoes, which shows up as a green tinge on skin. You can still use the potato, but remove the green part first.

- To store asparagus for up to three days, remove the band and stand stalks upright in a large measuring cup filled with a couple of inches of water. Place a plastic bag over the top and refrigerate. You can store broccoli the same way for longer keeping.

- Store mushrooms in paper bags in the refrigerator. Avoid plastic bags; they make mushrooms slimy.

- Refrigerate fresh gingerroot in a plastic bag for up to two weeks. Note that it doesn't always have to be peeled before using. Read the recipe. (Freeze peelings in a plastic bag and use them to flavour Asian-style soups.)

- Freeze trimmings from onions, mushrooms, celery and carrots, along with parsley stems, overripe tomatoes, limp celery and a sprig of herb, in heavy-duty resealable bags. Make stock when you have enough – you can get about 2 L of stock from 1/2 lb (250 g) of trimmings. Avoid cabbage leaves (too strong-tasting) and potato trimmings, which cloud stock.

- Freeze tough and woody mushroom stems from exotic mushrooms like oyster, portobello and shiitake mushrooms. When you have enough, make mushroom-flavoured broth for a soup or use it in risotto instead of chicken stock.

A chef's grab bag of tips

- Resealable plastic bags are a wonderful invention. They're excellent for marinating, since they're nonreactive like glass or stainless steel, which means they won't create off-flavours or cause discolouration. And you can easily turn the meat, fish or poultry to expose all sides to the marinade. After use – toss! When you need a decorating bag for icing or melted chocolate, simply fill a small plastic bag, twist the top down to the contents, trim off a tiniest bit of the corner, then pipe. When filling plastic bags with cooled soups or stock, set bag in large measure for support, then fill and seal.

- Teas make an exotic ingredient. Think of Chinese green tea ice cream. Or our own Darjeeling Eggfree Eggnog (page 136) and Iced Lemon and Ginger Mint Tea (page 35), a twist on Morroccan iced mint tea, which is traditionally much sweeter. You can use leftover black tea as the liquid in a stew. Use coarsely ground coffee beans as well as tea bags to infuse cream with their flavour for custards or home-made ice creams.

- Crumbs – sweet or savoury – help jazz up food. We used creme sandwich cookie crumbs to dress up a cheesecake (see page 109), and you can use gingersnaps to dress up fresh peaches. Brush peeled ripe peach halves with unsalted butter and grill; fill with goat cheese and sprinkle with crumbled gingersnaps. For breading foods, crush some corn flakes! The following will yield 1 cup (250 mL) crumbs: 10 *PC 'Eat the Middle First!'* Chocolate Vanilla Creme Cookies, 8 *PC* English-Style Gingersnap Cookies, 9 *PC* Swedish Crisp Toasts, 3 cups (750 mL) *PC* Corn Flakes. Graham cracker crumbs are widely available, and great for sprinkling between layers of pudding or on top as a garnish.

- Soften rock-hard ice cream in your microwave oven. Microwave 2 L on High for 15 to 20 seconds. To get a jump on serving ice cream to a crowd, scoop it in advance and freeze the scoops on a tray. You can get about 45 scoops from 2 L.

- Frozen phyllo is extremely easy to work with, but it must be completely thawed first so that it doesn't crack and break. (Refrigerated phyllo found in ethnic stores is less fragile but also thicker, so there is a tradeoff.) Transfer frozen phyllo to the refrigerator the day before using. Don't worry if phyllo pastry does tear during shaping; tears don't show and they only add to the texture.

- If a turkey or pie is browning too quickly, grab the aluminum foil. It's a dandy troubleshooter. Tear off a sheet, lightly punch it in the middle to create a bit of a "tent" and place this tent over the surface you're trying to protect.

A Thanksgiving bonus – turkey stock

When the Thanksgiving turkey is stripped after the feast, the fun begins. You have the carcass to make stock from – the perfect base for soups. If you don't make the stock immediately, then freeze the bones for when you have time.

After removing turkey meat for sandwiches or casseroles, break up the carcass and add the pieces to a large stockpot. (If you stuffed the turkey, you can leave some of the clingy bits inside; they will add flavour and body to the stock.) Cover carcass with cold water. Add one onion, three allspice berries if you have them (they add a subtle difference), and six whole black peppercorns (long cooking makes ground pepper turn bitter). Bring to a boil; lower heat, cover and simmer for 2 to 3 hours to extract the most flavour. Occasionally remove the scum that floats to the surface. After removing from heat, lift out the turkey bones with tongs, then strain the stock in batches to remove remaining solids. Make a soup or cool the stock to room temperature, then refrigerate for up to 3 days, or freeze for longer storage. Stock can be frozen in convenient 1- or 2-cup amounts in plastic freezer bags for sauces, soups or risotto.

(What to do with cranberry sauce left over from a turkey dinner? Mix it with an equal amount of *PC Gourmet Barbecue Sauce*, and brush it over pork loin or chicken pieces before roasting.)

Don't let the bones from a roasted chicken from the hot deli pass you by, either. They're good for stock, too. Cook immediately or freeze the bones in a resealable heavy-duty plastic bag. Over the next few weeks, if they're in the freezer that long, add parsley stems (they don't discolour stock as much as the leaves do), pieces of onion (not the brown skin, which adds colour but can also leave a bitter taste) and carrot to the bag. When you're ready to make stock, empty the frozen contents of the bag into a large saucepot, cover with cold water and bring to a boil. Reduce the heat and simmer for about 2 hours.

Glossary of cooking terms

Boil – bring liquid to boiling point. Water boils at 212°F (100°C).

Braise – cook food at low temperatures, covered, in some liquid on the stove or in the oven.

Chop – cut into pieces 1/4 inch or less.

Dice – cut into 1/4-inch cubes.

Julienne – cut into thin strips about the size of matchsticks.

Parboil – boil briefly. This can be anywhere from 30 seconds if you want to loosen the skin of tomatoes and peaches, for example, or only as long as it takes water to return to a boil, if you're trying to bring up the colour of green vegetables. Parboiling potatoes and other root vegetables for a few minutes helps cut roasting time.

Purée – put food through blender or food processor, or sieve, until smooth.

Reduce – cook until reduced in volume and thickened.

Simmer – cook below boiling point. Bubbles will form and slowly break.

Sauté – pan-fry quickly in a bit of butter or oil.

Strain – separate liquids and solids by passing through a sieve.

Index